Neither Liberal nor Conservative be

An Action Plan for People Disgusted by Polarized Politics

LARRY R. BRADLEY

KINDRED MINDS
ENTERPRISES

Omaha, Nebraska

Library of Congress Control Number: 2006931724
ISBN-10: 0-9788290-0-X
ISBN-13: 978-0-97882-900-1

Publisher's Cataloging-in-Publication

Bradley, Larry R. (Larry Ross)
   Neither liberal nor conservative be : an action plan
  for people disgusted by polarized politics / by Larry R.
  Bradley.
   p. cm.
  Includes bibliographical references and index.

   1. Political participation--United States.
  2. Polarization (Social sciences) 3. Political parties--
United States. 4. Political culture--United States.
I. Title.

JK1764.B73 2006   323'.042'0973
        QBI06-600317

Cover Design by Lisa Pelto
Desktop production of Jennifer Frazier, ideasinc.
Editorial services of Write On, Inc.
Marketing and Publicity Concierge Marketing Inc.
Illustrator Jack Cassady

Kindred Minds Enterprises
663 North 132nd Street, Suite 125
Omaha, NE 68154
www.KindredMindsEnt.com
Printed in the United States of America.
10 9 8 7 6 5 4 3 2

Contents

Acknowledgments

I write this book hoping to create a better future for my two daughters and in memory of their mother, my first wife.

This book would not be possible without the love and support of my wife, Gail.

Thanks also to family, friends, co-workers and superiors for their love, friendship, support and contributions.

In order to bring this book to you, Kindred Minds Enterprises needed the help of several professionals, whom I acknowledge here.

Lisa Pelto with Concierge Marketing uses her over 20 years' experience in the publishing industry to help authors succeed, especially when they must navigate the minefield of self publishing. Her Web site is at **www.conciergemarketing.com.**

Glenn Davis, a professional journalist and former lobbyist, has generously gone above and beyond to personally offer not just business advice, but to edit the work in progress. His advice and encouragement have been invaluable.

John R. (Jack) Cassady is a retired Army officer and combat veteran. He's also a professional cartoonist whose works have been in print since the 1970s. He has kindly produced the illustrations in this book. A truer patriot you will not find. His Web site is **www.toonmaker.com.**

Brian Massey, a former co-worker and 100 percent great guy created the matrix charts.

The Kindred Minds Enterprises logo was developed by the superb work of Damon Anderson of Creative Reservoir. His Web site is **www.creativereservoir.com**.

Thanks also to the many other unnamed professionals who have lent their time and talent to make this book a reality.

Larry R. Bradley

☑

Introduction

At election time, do you choose between the lesser of two evils?

Do you ask yourself, "Is **this** the best we can do?"

Does polarized American politics disgust you?

Does the inability to solve our national issues drive you crazy?

Do you wish you could do something to clean up this mess, but then you immediately trip over thoughts like these?

- Where could I begin? (The issues are just too complex.)

- What's wrong?

- Why are things so vicious and antagonistic?

- Where is the reasoned voice of wisdom to show me the way?

- Who has the time to figure out **the** solution? Not me.

- The whole business is so slimy and disgusting,
  it repulses me.

- And, anyway, what impact can one person have?

If these are your feelings, then this book is what you've
been looking for.

This open letter to the American political parties gives you
a way to fight back.

I am writing this book as I might write a letter to car makers
not producing the car I am willing to buy. Although I don't
expect one of them will give me 100 percent of what I want,
I would hope one of them would give me 85 to 90 percent
of my needs for performance and comfort. In the same way,
no major political party is promoting the policies and candidates or taking actions I can agree with 85 to 90 percent of
the time. This book is my way of telling the parties my opinion
of what they must offer in order to consistently receive my
vote. My hope is that you, the reader, will join me in saying
this is the kind of politics and government we want.

I believe changing the policies and candidates of political
parties is important, because the parties, through their policies
and elected candidates, ultimately determine the government
activities that impact our lives and the lives of the people we
love.

Phrasing my purpose another way: If I were a government
agency, I would look at this book as a Request for Proposal
(RFP). The government issues RFPs when they need a solution
for a problem so unique that nothing currently exists to solve

that problem. An RFP allows the government to start with a fresh sheet of paper to find new solutions beyond inadequate existing ones. In this situation, none of our current political parties is providing me the promise of the kind of government I want. I am, therefore, writing a proposal for the kind of political party I want with the hope many of you will agree with my vision. Together we can change how this country does its political business.

Why read this book?

Because this book will provide you a new way to have a voice and a new vote to encourage our political parties to bring both long-term progress and prosperity to our political process and our country. If you are dissatisfied with the choices you have in the voting booth, then this book will help you understand why you are dissatisfied. Further, you will be provided a means to voice those dissatisfactions and get the changes you want.

Making a further comparison to car makers, consider this. If any manufacturer sees an opportunity to outsell its competitors, the manufacturer will take it, especially if that opportunity brings with it the potential for long-term dominance over the competition. If enough people like you will . . .

- **Read** this book
- **Agree** with the principles proposed and
- **Tell** the political parties the one of them that offers

policies and candidates in agreement with those principles will be the one for whom you vote-

. . . then the political parties must act to become dominant or be dominated.

Why have I written this book?

I write because I can no longer carry these ideas inside me, for two reasons. First, I have recently lost too many people who were close to me, and their deaths remind me I have no guarantees on how long I have in this world. I want these ideas debated and used to beat back the forces of stupidity, narrow-mindedness and shortsightedness, whatever the source. Second, I find those same negative forces are creating a world I do not want my children to inherit. My hopes are for changes that will benefit others for generations to come.

What's different about my approach?

In my research I've found every published offering dedicated to the proposition that the liberal or (vice versa) conservative point of view is absolutely correct in all cases and here is why the opposing point of view is wrong. You won't get that here.

Instead, my approach begins with a discussion of how our underlying beliefs and desires relate to the world around us. I show you how to build on a common ground of consensus and defend yourself from those who benefit from divisiveness.

The language of American politics used at the turn of the 21st century has become perverted and polarized. Reasonable people seem unable to have objective discussions of our problems. As a result, our problems keep getting worse.

This book is about what we can do individually and collectively to get back to objective discussions and problem solving. Here's an illustration that explains this thought.

> A magnetic compass tells you with absolute certainty which direction north is. But a compass doesn't work well, however, around magnets. Put a magnet next to a compass and "ping!" – the northward pointing arrow snaps over to the magnet, and you can't tell which direction north truly is.

Today, the same thing happens in our political discussions when an objective argument is not going well for one side or the other. The losing side is likely to confuse the direction of the discussion by magnetizing that discussion with emotion-generating terms such as liberal or neo-con. In fact, the term liberal today has been so successfully polarized by its opposition that the word is often said with the same spit-it-out distaste as child molester.

What's more, people today are likely to discuss political topics by mimicking the same approach they hear on television and radio, little realizing what is heard from the media is a form of theater. In theater, conflict enhances drama, and drama attracts an audience who, advertisers hope, will buy products or services. So, using the same language you hear on radio and television invites conflict instead of consensus in your discussions.

What I seek to do, therefore, is to provide you a usable analytical framework without these conditions. Within this new structure, issues can be objectively analyzed without blame and prejudice, thereby developing a working political philosophy you can embrace. You may suddenly realize you have not really had a philosophy of your own. Now you will.

Successful people are successful not because they don't have problems. They are successful because they confront the reality of their problems and find a way to turn their circumstances to their advantage. As a member of the voting public, you can too!

Let me show you how this analysis can be applied. Using that analytical framework, let me describe alternative positions on some of the more contentious issues of our time. Do I expect that you will agree with me 100 percent? No, but I do expect you will be able to approach these topics with more clarity and insight and more ably resist manipulation.

My means of providing the framework to you is by relating politics to everyday life experiences. The experiences will be common ones, such as buying a car and talking about sports. The idea is to use your understanding of everyday life to relate to a political topic you may not understand.

Are we missing the target?

Here's another example of what I'm trying to do.

Before a hunter hunts with a rifle, the hunter must "sight it in." The military calls this "zeroing" a weapon. Zeroing means that the user of the weapon performs a series of systematic mechanical adjustments and then tests those adjustments by firing at a close-in target. The adjustments synchronize the sights of the weapon with the actual firing mechanism for the particular human being using the weapon. These adjustments are done to insure that, when the weapon is fired, the projectile will go to the exact place where the weapon is aimed.

If the rifle is fired and the target is missed, the miss does not mean that the rifle, the sights or the firer is defective and worthy of blame and derision. The miss only means the three have not yet achieved alignment.

Realize that a small mistake in aim at a short distance translates to a large mistake in aim at a long distance. Remember the geometry you learned in school? A mistake of just one degree at the point of origin will put you off target by 100 meters for a target 1,000 meters away. When you "get your zero," your bullets (your arguments for or against a given topic) go where you want them to go. Losing your "argument zero" may mean your issue bullets may miss your audience.

I contend we have "lost our zero" in political conversation and debate. We have lost the common ingredient for civil objective discussion. We no longer have a common understanding (alignment, if you will) of our political objectives and the terms and their definitions used to debate the means of achieving those objectives. I hope this book helps us to "get our zero" in political dialogue so we can move forward in our discussion of issues with intelligence and reason.

Positioning our views

Another way of building consensus is to be open to more information, ideas and points of view. As in my example of using a compass, imagine you're in the desert and don't know exactly where you are. You can use the compass to find the direction from where you now stand to a known point in the distance such as a mountain peak or a television antenna. You then plot that direction on a map. Knowing one distant point will get you within 1,000 meters of your true location. Knowing two points will get you within 100 meters. Knowing three points brings you within 10 meters. The Global Positioning System (GPS) works on the same principle using satellites.

Shouldn't the same process apply to topical debate? Isn't the more information introduced a good thing? If the power and logic of your ideas is good, then shouldn't they be able to withstand the challenge of other ideas? Could some people and groups resist other ideas because they fear their ideas will be exposed as inadequate and, therefore, rejected?

One of the few constants in life is change itself. The issues confronting us have no simple answers and all will require adjustment as time moves on. Setting policy can be compared to the setting of the sail on a ship. As someone once told me, "The problem with setting policy and writing laws is not in having the intended effect you want. The problem is in avoiding the unintended effect. When you throw that big rock in the water to make that big splash, you have to consider whose boat you're going to rock with the resulting waves rippling out from the impact."

Former President Lyndon Johnson is quoted as saying as much, "You do not examine legislation in light of the benefits it will convey if properly administered, but in the light of the wrongs it would do and the harms it would cause if improperly administered."

I invite you to share your thoughts and add any perspectives I may have missed at my Web site: **www.KindredMindsEnt.com**.

Are you ready to influence the political process for the better?

Part I
Refining Your Political Philosophy

ONE
WHAT IS YOUR POLITICAL PHILOSOPHY?

If you were asked, "What is your political philosophy?" how would you reply?

Would you say, "I'm a Republican," "I'm a Democrat," "I'm a Liberal," "I'm a Conservative," or would you say, "I just vote for the best candidate"? You might even say, "I don't really have a philosophy of my own. I've never thought about it."

If you say you're a Republican or Democrat, don't you really have an affiliation? Is there a philosophy that causes you to have that affiliation? If you say you're a Liberal or Conservative, then exactly what is your philosophy? Without simply reciting a list of issues you support or oppose, in 50 words or less, tell me what liberal or conservative means to you. Remember the old saying, words don't have meaning, people do. If you say you vote for the "best candidate," then what criteria (in other words, philosophy) do you use to make that choice?

After reading this book, you may start to develop for the

first time your own unique individual political philosophy. The two major political parties in this country are on their own unlikely to offer you what I offer: a school of thought made of common sense and moderation that may have been at the back of your own mind for some time. The pressures of daily life demand your time and energy, preventing your full development of this philosophy. Knowing that fact, zealots at the opposing ends of the political spectrum will be most unhappy you are reading this book. Those zealots don't want you reading something counter to their own school of thought. People with knowledge are much more difficult to manipulate. At the end of this book, you'll be able to communicate with the key members of the political world and tell them this is the philosophy (with some personal changes you no doubt want to voice) you want to see applied to how your government works.

Why should the major political parties care about this book and your opinion of it? Because, like any passionate competitors in war or business, the political parties want not just to survive, they want to win and, even more, to leave no survivors to fight another day. If one party perceives another party is about to take possession of a political capability that overcomes all other capabilities in the winning of elections, then the other party will be forced to either get that capability for themselves or find a counter to it. If enough of you read this book and then tell politically influential people that the party and candidates who share this book's philosophy are the ones for whom you will vote, then you are proposing the capability that a party must have to survive and win elections.

You will disagree with some aspects of this book. That's okay. Just take the time, maturity and wisdom to realize this: Someone on the other end of the political spectrum agrees with the proposed position just as passionately as you disagree. When you disagree, challenge yourself to question your basic assumptions.

The author, lecturer and business consultant Brian Tracy counsels his students to say, "I may be wrong. I often am." Tracy further counsels that the people or companies that continue to move forward to greater success and profitability are the ones, when confronted with difficulties, willing to go back and look at the basic assumptions they made that put them on that course of action. When they find those assumptions flawed, they make needed adjustments.

Didn't people used to think that the earth was flat and that the sun revolved around the earth? Weren't those beliefs proven wrong? Then maybe we need to apply this process to some of the ongoing issues that divide us. After all, **isn't the ultimate goal to find those solutions that serve the largest number of people for the longest period of time balanced with doing the least harm or disruption to the least number of people and at the same time be the best solution monetarily for the funds available among competing priorities?** Finding those solutions likely means you must then search beyond the competing ideologies of the Extreme Right and the Extreme Left.

Part One of this book will describe four understandable ways for you to develop a position on political issues in the

U.S. in the early part of the 21st century. Developing a position or philosophy on political issues at this time can be likened to one or more of four everyday activities common in America today. Politics will be contrasted to sports, buying a car, being an innocent bystander in the middle of an argument and sailing. If you understand this common topic, you can then use that understanding to relate to a topic you may not fully understand.

In Part Two of this book, these analytical methods will be applied to some of the most contentious issues of our time so you can see how they work.

In Part Three and in the resources at the end of the book, you will be offered additional tools for continued study, a suggested letter for you to write, and a method for finding addresses for the people and organizations you'll want to send your letters.

One final thought before we begin: Somewhere, sometime, someone is going to tell me with a pitying look and a figurative condescending pat on the head how misguided I am and unknowledgeable of how things work in the real world. My reply is simple. I realize that politics is not done now in the way this book describes. I'm looking for the people who will do things the way this book recommends. If you happen to be an elected official, my message is this: If you can't or won't do things this way, then I intend to fire you and find someone who can.

The introduction is over. Let's begin.

Two
How Politics Is Like Sports

Analogy One: How Your Relationship to Politics Is Like Your Relationship to Sports

This book shows you how to use your understanding of sports to understand politics in each of the following ways:

First, is politics like a sport you don't care for? If so, then what impacts do you need to consider?*

Or, second, is politics like a sport you're interested in, but can't spare the time?

Or, third, is politics like a sport in which you're interested, but don't understand?**

---

* Don't be afraid of this book because you don't like sports or know a lot about sports. I will avoid using a lot of technical sports mumbo-jumbo the average person cannot understand. One way you might relate better to this first section is to substitute "type of music" for sports and specific musical types (pop, rap, country, for example) where I have named a specific sport.

** Later, I discuss three other comparisons of sports and politics:
  • Are there parallels between sports and political topics such as equal opportunity?
  • Are there parallels between sports and our foreign policy?
  • Are there parallels between the statistical detail sports fans possess and the statistical reality voters should demand to be applied to political policies and functions?

So, if **politics is like a sport you don't care for** realize the difference between not caring for a sport and not caring about politics. If you don't like World Cup Soccer, or baseball, or for that matter any other sport, then your only discomfort is likely to be some awkwardness at a social event where that particular sport is the primary focus. Your life will go on unaffected by who wins the game or championship. Unless you get caught in traffic outside a stadium or some possession of yours is damaged somehow in some post-victory celebration, you may not even be aware a sporting contest is going on. That's not the case with politics, however.

That's because politics is an eternal debate about four issues:

- How you will be governed (which impacts the freedom to live as you choose)

- On what you will be taxed (with which you may or may not agree)

- What your taxes will be used for (with which you may or may not agree)

- How much you will be taxed (which diverts money from your personal goals)

If you say you're not interested in politics, then you are saying you don't care about:

- How and in what manner you and those you love will be allowed to live now and in the future

- What the government can tax you on (cars, property, dividends, and the like)

- What governmental programs your tax money will fund

- How much you will have to pay in taxes to fund those programs (Of course, every dollar you pay in taxes is a dollar not available for your personal use.)

Even if you find politics uninteresting, you should at least appreciate why you should be aware of politics. Reading to this point, you might reply:

"Well, yes, I find politics uninteresting, but I feel I must do my duty to vote in the major elections that matter."

You might also say, **"Well, I do find politics interesting, but I don't have time for it.** I keep up as much as I can. I vote in major elections that matter."

Or, third, you might say, **"Well, I do find politics interesting, but I don't really understand it.** I try to understand as much as I can, but I have trouble making a choice when I vote. I vote in major elections that matter."

If one of these describes you, then you may want to consider this point. If you don't like a sport, or have time for it, or not understand it, then you may not watch the whole season, but you may show up and watch the championship series. That's not a bad approach to sports, but it's a bad idea in politics. Here's why.

In the United States the political system has political parties with either primaries or a caucus process. Parties select candidates to seek office. The people who are involved in that selection process are passionate. Because they truly like politics, they devote their time to it and understand it. Those with an extreme ideology will attempt to nominate people to run for office who have that same extremeness of ideology. The primary election season for political candidates is the same thing as training camp or spring training in sports. Here is the place and time you pick the players to represent you in the regular season final competition (in other words, the general election). What's more, the players you pick will determine your style of play. As a football fan, you may prefer to have a team with a particular style of offense. But if you don't have a coach leading the team who will find and develop the people and play to support that style, then your offense will likely be focused on what you consider to be boring.

Now, as a voter, what does that mean to you?

Have you ever gotten to the week before a general election, tried to decide which candidate to vote for and found both candidates too ideologically extreme for you? The likely reason is that the more moderately balanced candidates were defeated during the party's internal selection process. The zealots with the extreme ideology got their people in for the general election because they showed up for the primary elections or caucuses. If you want more moderately balanced candidates, then you must show up during the primary elections or caucuses. There are a couple of other relatively easy things you can do.

Let's play ball

Pair with someone who shares your outlook on life and politics with the goal of knowing what each of the major political parties is planning, saying and doing. If you're married, then you might register as a Democrat and your spouse as a

Republican. (You can always switch back before a primary or a caucus.) You can also make a small monetary contribution to each of the two parties. That way your house will receive literature from each party for you to compare and analyze. You will also be more likely to be selected for the surveys the parties and candidates conduct to develop policy positions. Imagine the impact this could have. How demoralizing to the zealots to find their extreme position not enjoying widespread support! Wouldn't the zealots be forced to find broader consensus policies and candidates?

Thinking ahead, you might ask, "Won't this give us bland politics with both parties offering the same approach to our political issues?" The answer is no. As a baseball manager, wouldn't it be your goal to have a roster where every player was capable of a high "batting average"? Don't you want every batter to hit every time and advance around the bases as far as possible? Don't you want players with great fielding and throwing skills? With agreed upon goals, isn't the question which players are the best overall players?

Translating that to politics, if the basic political policy objectives are uniformly accepted, then isn't the question which candidate is the most qualified and offers the best ideas to achieve those objectives?

For a moment, let's get even more basic. Have you ever thought about why you don't like a particular sport? People don't like a sport for many reasons, but one of them may be that they don't see themselves competing in a sport. Maybe you have poor hand-eye coordination and you don't like baseball because you could never play the game well as a child. If you can't compete well, then you don't want to participate. That's only natural.

Similarly, another reason you may not like politics is that politics to you is a lot of arguing, and you don't like or you don't want to argue with people. That's another value of this book. When you hear someone saying something you disagree with (by virtue of having read this book), you don't have to confront that person directly. Instead, you can say, "That's very interesting. Have you read *Neither Liberal Nor Conservative Be?*" If the person says yes, then you can ask what they think of the reasoning described here. If the person has read the book, then you should be able to have a reasoned discussion. If the person has not read the book, then you can recommend they read it and then re-contact you for discussion.

If the person presses you to describe the reasoning in the book, then you have the option to describe the reasoning yourself or to say you don't think you can do the idea justice and suggest again that the other person read the book for themselves. That way you avoid confrontation and you contribute to reasoned dialogue and education leading to consensus rather than conflict. (You may find this particularly useful in dealing with people whose means of discussing political issues is repeating the confrontational language they've heard on radio and television.)

Three other aspects of relating sports to politics will be discussed later. For now, let's go on our next analogy.

THREE
How Politics Is Like Buying a Car

Analogy Two: How Developing a Position on a Political Issue Is Like Buying a Car

Imagine yourself shopping for a car. Cars have characteristics such as engine size, transmission capability, overall functionality (sports car vs. pickup truck) and a host of other features that matter to you. When you analyze what you want in a car, let's assume you conclude (for purposes of this example) only two manufacturers offer the long-term capability and durability you want.

When you really get into the details, you find the models of the two manufacturers seem almost identical to you. You may feel that where one manufacturer's model is strong, that advantage is cancelled by a weakness in another area. In an attempt to decide between the two, you visit both their car lots. There for the first time you truly see the problem in trying to choose between the two models. No matter which vehicle you're considering, every vehicle has a monkey head mounted on the front of the car like a hood ornament or on the trunk like a spoiler. The question you ask yourself is, **"Why can't I get one of these cars without a monkey head on it?"**

Why are you thinking this? Because one of the reasons for choosing one car rather than another is that the car's styling is a reflection of who you are as an individual. The car represents you to the world with regard to your values on a variety of topics. The presence of a monkey's head on our fictional political cars is not a representation of who you are, and so that fact complicates your choice.

At this point, your question may be, **"I understand what you mean about a monkey's head as a hood ornament and how it could affect my choice for an automobile, but how does that relate to politics?"** Here's how.

To attract a larger number of voters, political parties are going to offer proposed policy positions to attract people from groups unlike the one you are normally a part of. Those proposed positions, because of your lack of familiarity with these groups, may seem to you unreasonable and even offensive. Just remember, some positions you advocate may seem equally unreasonable and offensive to them. These proposed policies in politics are the equivalent of monkey heads on cars.

To repeat, **if you are asking yourself politically, "Can't I get a car without a monkey's head?" probably the answer is "Yes, you can for the car you buy, but you may have to accept one on cars other people drive."**

Instead of being able to find a political party without monkey heads, you are going to have to study each party's monkey-head proposals and decide which party's monkey heads you will reject and which you will tolerate. A party with too many negative monkey-head attributes is probably the one you will vote against.

So how do you decide which party's monkey heads to reject and which to tolerate? And deciding to reject is the more likely way you will choose. A common political wisdom is that people don't vote **for** something. They vote **against** something.

Knowing this, the two major political parties will try to win by making sure you are aware of the other parties' monkey heads. In fact, you can count on each party to magnify the size of the monkey heads of the other party in your view –

raising your blood pressure and your emotions in an attempt to make their own party seem more desirable. In other words, one party will attempt to win by causing you to reject the other. In the process, issues of substance that affect you personally are largely ignored in order to focus on the monkey-head issues.

One way to choose: When you look at the issue more closely you see that the party offering the monkey head on behalf of a selected voter group is doing so as a sort of after-market product. In other words, the party is not **requiring** you to have a monkey's head on your car. The party is merely **advocating** that **those who wish to** have monkey's heads mounted on their vehicles be allowed to do so. That may make monkey's heads more acceptable to you. Or so it seems.

To confirm that allowing others to mount monkey heads on their vehicles is something tolerable to you, you may also want to ask yourself these questions:

Will there be any negative ripple effects from allowing this policy?

For example, if this policy would allow the beheading of monkeys in order to create the ornaments, then that's probably a bad idea. Does that mean that monkeys would be bred for beheading? It's especially a bad idea if monkeys were an endangered species. Moreover, rotting monkey heads smell bad and attract flies and other vermin. If the heads were replicas made out of inanimate materials that wouldn't decompose, then that's probably okay.

As a real-world example, consider this: You may recognize there are, unfortunately, people in this world who are sexually aroused by children. The overwhelming majority of members of society, however, consider this a perversion and will not allow a policy that would legitimate such behavior. That would be an intolerable monkey-head issue. If you are considering under what conditions you would accept a monkey-head type of issue whose appeal or lack of appeal is not nearly so clear, then you may also want to ask the following question.

Are you (or a specific group of people already in existence who are unable to defend themselves) severely harmed by this policy?

- Physically?
- Mentally/emotionally?
- Monetarily?

If there is no harm, there is no foul. If the answer to all these questions is no, then you are probably looking at being able to exercise a personal choice that does not impact you. There should be no reason, therefore, to oppose the exercise of that personal choice. When the answer to some or all of the questions is yes, then allowing a policy proposal to become an actual policy requires more scrutiny and may not be allowed at all.

Does allowing such a policy set a precedent that opens the door to the creation of another policy that is unacceptable to you?

Could this, for example, lead to the mounting of water buffalo heads, which obstruct the driver's vision and are unsafe? Could this lead to a minority (should the group gain control of the political process) requiring you to mount a monkey head on your own automobile, whether you want to or not? Depending on the nature of the "monkey's head" as a political issue, this could be decisive on your position.

So, summarizing at this point, our political philosophy is this: We are on guard to keep ourselves from becoming so distracted by cultural monkey-head issues we fail to assess properly which party and its candidates offer us the best potential for competence in governing. We recognize the inevitability of monkey-head issues. Monkey-head issues are not usually considered to be issues of substance for us as intelligent, involved citizens and voters unless the issue impacts us negatively in some way in a ripple effect that is physical, mental/emotional or financial or sets a precedent that could lead to a future negative impact that is physical, mental/emotional or financial.

Further, as voters and citizens, we are saying we want our political parties and candidates to offer us solutions to issues of substance. Political parties should avoid monkey-head issues that affect us negatively physically, mentally/emotionally, or financially or which offered a means of setting a precedent that will later be used to institute a policy that affects us negatively, as previously described. We understand that political parties may offer monkey-head policy proposals as a means of attracting additional voters to them.

We can be accepting of those policy proposals as long as their impact on us is minimal physically, mentally/emotionally, or financially and are not structured to yield negative ripple effects or as a means of setting a precedent to be used later to institute a policy that affects us negatively.

Put more simply, it is okay to offer a group unlike our own the option to indulge in a form of behavior of its choosing that we would not choose for ourselves as long we can choose not to do that behavior. Offering a group unlike our own the means of forcing on us the adoption of behavior we would not choose for ourselves is not okay unless a very compelling case can be made for the goodness of that behavior.

We further want our political parties and candidates to avoid using monkey-head issues as a smokescreen to mask an agenda lacking substance in such priority areas as security and prosperity or that contain positions on issues of substance we do not favor.

See the Resources for an example of how to use these principles when you find yourself involved in an actual discussion of an issue with someone.

Four
Developing a Political Philosophy for Unavoidable Conflicts

Analogy Three: Developing a Position on a Political Issue Mirrors Being an Innocent Bystander in the Middle of a Conflict

Comparing politics to buying a car illustrates that many issues can be analyzed with a propensity to live and let live. One would like to believe that the majority of us want to get along with those around us and live in a nation that embraces the widest degree of freedom and choice possible. Unfortunately, we will always live among individuals and groups who do not share that outlook. This chapter, therefore, is about dealing with political groups that insist you have their monkey head on your car.

Refer to the following illustration and consider this:

Imagine you're living in a town down in the valley next to the river. Life is good in the town. Life is being lived with intelligence, abundance and tolerance. But suddenly, two warring armies arrive on the opposing hillsides above the town, trying to destroy one another. Each army is shooting artillery at the other. Neither side's artillery is able to shoot far enough to hit the army on the other hillside, so their shells fall and explode among those in the valley. The two armies' inability to shoot far enough doesn't matter though, because to win the war neither army actually has to destroy the other. The rule is this: The army able to get enough people from the town to come up on that army's hill so it has 51 percent of the total population wins.

Those who live in the valley who want peace have a choice. Their first choice for peace is to be intimidated or misled into joining one of the two armies. The second choice for peace – those who live in the valley must march up each hill and defeat each of the opposing armies. The valley dwellers must destroy the two armies' cannon and take away the ability to make more cannons. They must weigh in on the issue causing the conflict and resolve it once and for all. Otherwise, the life they enjoy, the life with intelligence, abundance and tolerance, will be a distant memory for them and their children.

Polling of American voters reveals the majority live in the valley politically with a live-and-let-live approach that encourages and values intelligence, abundance and tolerance. The difficulty is that a minority of American voters want to live according to an extreme social philosophy they want implemented through political activism. Essentially, there are two extreme philosophies opposing one another. Their supporters form two armies in constant conflict becoming a hindrance to peace, prosperity and harmony. These two armies don't care that you will accept a monkey's head on their cars as an option. That's not good enough for them. They demand that you have a monkey's head on your car whether you want one or not and nothing less will do for them.

What we're attempting to illustrate with an analogy of armies firing artillery is this. When election time comes, these two extreme groups set up their cannon in the form of attack ads, Internet email campaigns and other means of negative campaigning. Their goal is not really to achieve a broad consensus for harmonious governing. Their goal is to gain just enough votes that will give them the power to pursue a very narrow agenda. Your goal as a voter is to be able to resist the manipulation and intimidation by clearly knowing your values and how to interpret the issues before the artillery starts.

As the parents of misbehaving children sometimes must assert their authority, so must the voters who "live in the valley." Valley-dwelling voters must decide how they want an issue resolved and then let the "misbehaving children" know that what they want is unreasonable, that they may not have it and to shut up about it. For example, an interest group might be told that they may not mandate the mounting of monkey heads on automobiles. If the interest group wants to demonstrate to the world how short-sighted, ignorant and immature they are, then the interest group is welcome to mount a monkey head on their own cars. But such is not for the valley dwellers.

There are real-world examples of "monkey heads" in American history. America had to fight a civil war to resolve slavery. America had to institute a constitutional amendment to give women the right to vote. America had to rescind a constitutional amendment regarding the prohibition of alcohol in the United States. (Some readers may be too young to remember this contentious issue; too young, even, to remember the television show or the movie about how Elliot Ness and the Untouchables came to fame. Prohibition may seem especially unbelievable today, given the large number of ads for beer and other forms of alcoholic beverages in all sorts of media. But a minority in our society were able to maneuver themselves into sufficient political power to forbid the sale of alcoholic beverages in this country.)

These examples speak to the fact that voters must stand up to these zealots and their issues. Slavery and the sale of alcohol are not issues today. In essence, they were finally settled in a public way. Do these issues still boil below the surface in certain ways? Yes. Slavery boils (or at least simmers) in the form of race relations. But no one could seriously consider trying to reintroduce the institution of slavery into everyday American society. Slavery is a dead issue. And while you are free to attempt to influence the choices of people in not drinking alcohol or in drinking responsibly, the matter of whether or not alcoholic beverages can be sold in America is a dead issue.

Like slavery and prohibition, America has other issues today (such as abortion, stem cell research and same-sex marriage) that have yet to be resolved. In subsequent chapters the criteria established in Part One will be used to examine some of those issues – issues that have been vexing us long enough. If America wishes itself progress, then today's equivalents of slavery and prohibition must be put to rest.

It is not my purpose to tell you what to believe. My purpose is to show you ways to discover what you do believe. Moreover, I want to show you ways not only to know what you believe, but why you believe it. Knowing what you believe and why you believe it will help you see whether the candidates and parties, through their policies and actions, share your beliefs. My personal belief – my hope and my wish – is that the more of you who read this book and apply its concepts, the more this country will move from polarized political conflict to consensus.

With that said, I want to show you the next step in establishing your political philosophy.

What do people say about you?

Imagine that you have died and your soul is floating above your casket where you are able to hear people talk about you as a parent, friend, lover, wage-earner, citizen, and so forth. What kinds of words do you want said to describe you?

- Generous or Greedy?
- Open-minded or Close-minded?
- Intelligent or Ignorant?
- Far-seeing or Foolish?
- Mind Your Own Business or Meddling?
- Compassionate or Unfeeling?
- Loving or Hateful

For myself (and I hope for most of you), I would want the first set of word or words in each choice to be said of me. Now consider this chart:

	Socially Tolerant	Socially Intolerant
Fiscally Responsible		
Fiscally Irresponsible		

If you were required to characterize yourself by placing an "x" in one of the four quadrants, you would probably want to say you are socially tolerant (which means that you are more tolerant of the social views of others) and fiscally responsible (which means you are very practical with how you spend and save your money). After all, few people would want to be known as socially intolerant and fiscally irresponsible. Or, putting it in plainer terms, few people would want to be described as a racist bum. That means most people would make a mark in the diagram like this:

	Socially Tolerant	Socially Intolerant
Fiscally Responsible	X Position most likely preferred by individuals	
Fiscally Irresponsible		

During the latter half of the 20th century, applying these criteria to popular perceptions of the two major political parties would probably result in the following characterizations. The Democratic party would have an "x" somewhere in the lower left. Its members would be seen as advocates of the "little guy," the poor and minorities, but also the fiscally irresponsible masters of "tax and spend." The Republican party, on the other hand, would have its "x" in the upper right square of the quadrant. Republicans would be seen as socially intolerant and uncaring of poor people, but tightfisted in spending tax money, which gave them high marks for fiscal responsibility.

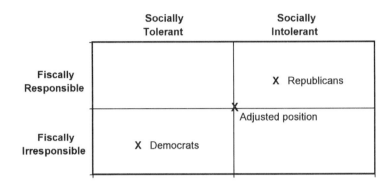

For the most part, however, the leaders of the two parties near the end of the 20th century were intelligent pragmatists and found common ground by moving toward the center of the chart. Ross Perot's campaign for the Presidency clearly illustrated the dangers of continued deficits on the economy, which moved the Democrats toward fiscal responsibility and the Republicans' discovery of how much people found programs like Medicare to be desirable and beneficial moved that party toward social tolerance.

These charts illustrate **why you may feel you are choosing between the lesser of two evils when you vote.** Earlier I said that a figurative question you may be asking yourself is "Why can't I get a car without a monkey head?" With this additional information we now change that question to **"Why isn't there a political party that offers me both social tolerance and fiscal responsibility?"**

The values you may want to apply in your personal life and in your politics are in the upper left quadrant. Unfortunately, neither party's basic philosophy is near your own. If you choose one party, then you may get social tolerance, but you're not getting the fiscal responsibility you're looking for, or vice versa. Whatever quality a party lacks becomes a monkey head for you and each party has one.

To reiterate, that means you have to choose which party's monkey heads you will accept and which you will reject. If you're in a place in your life where money matters are paramount to you, then you will be more likely to choose the party that gives you fiscal responsibility. If you place more emphasis on social issues, then you will be more likely to choose the party emphasizing social tolerance. By understanding these factors, you are also better equipped for approaching the two parties and asking for adjustments to their political (monkey-head) issues.

Let their political leadership know that you feel there should be

(a) no monkey's head at all or

(b) only an optional monkey's head or

(c) a monkey's head must be optional and allowed only if the further option to allow elephant's heads is clearly prohibited (or whatever other precedent-setting opportunity you feel needs to be prohibited if you allow the monkey-head proposal to be approved).

Building from the previous example, let's examine a more detailed set of matrix charts you may find useful in developing your personal political philosophy and determining your position on political parties and issues.

Principle-Centered Politics vs. Self-Interest Politics

Let me show you how to use the "monkey head" and "living in the valley" analogies, along with the matrices, to pick out whether a party and its candidates are offering you consistent principle-centered politics or inconsistent self-interest politics.

Isn't consistency one of the ideals you value in your dealings with the world around you? Have you ever thought about why fast food franchise chains have flourished in the USA? One answer is consistency. Whether in Sacramento, California, or Raleigh, North Carolina, if you go to a McDonald's (or a Wendy's or a Subway or a Burger King), you expect a consistent experience. For the money you are willing to pay, you expect to get the taste you want in food served with the timeliness you desire in the clean and well-lighted atmosphere you require.

If you're a parent, you strive to be consistent with your children. You may, for example, spend the same amount of money on each child for birthdays. If you help your oldest child have a car as they reach driving age, then you feel bound (all other things being equal) to help your other children when they reach that age.

So, just as you may reward a franchise fast food place for its consistency (especially when you find yourself in questionable surroundings), shouldn't you also create the expectation by a political party that you will reward consistent adherence to principles you value by voting for that party in uncertain times?

Given the fast-food analogy, here is how you can use a matrix to judge consistency to political principles you value.

Government and politics are rarely about choosing one value over another. Rather, **government and politics are about balancing competing values.** For example, how do you balance the rights of the government to mandate behavior versus the rights of the individual to make his or her own choices? A modified matrix illustrates this concept on the following pages.

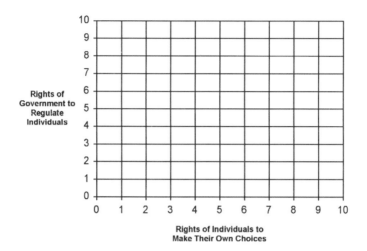

This matrix goes beyond the simple four-quadrant illustration shown before. This new matrix has 10 points on the "x" or horizontal axis (Rights of Individuals to make their own choices) and 10 points on the "y" or vertical axis (Rights of the Government to Regulate Individuals).

The rule in using this type of matrix is that the total value between the x and the y axis may not total more than 10 points. Why 10 points? Because totaling a score of more than 10 points is impossible. You cannot have laws for the same issue that simultaneously give **both** the maximum freedom in personal choice **and** the absolute power for government to regulate your personal choice.

If you give all your value to Rights of the Individual and zero points to Rights of the Government, then the matrix would look like this next one. A good example we can use here of rights of the government to mandate behavior versus the rights of individuals to make their own choices is using cell phones while driving. If you believe that government should have no right to ban you from using your cell phone in any way you want while driving, then this chart shows your position (X10/Y0).

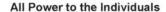

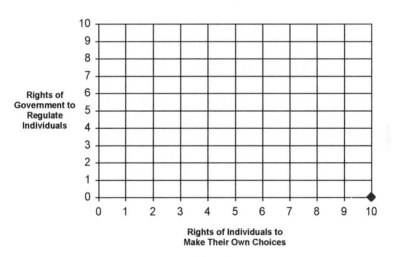

All Power to the Individuals

Reversing that, if you give zero value to Rights of the Individual and 10 points to Rights of the Government, then the matrix would look like the next chart (X0/Y10). If you believe that government has every right to ban you from using your cell phone in any way you choose while driving, then this chart shows your position.

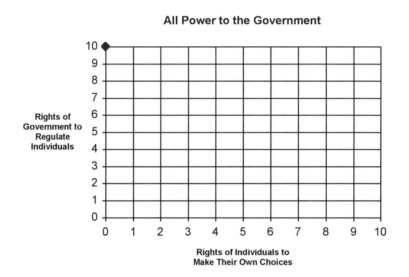

All Power to the Government

If you are someone who values balancing the two values equally by giving 5 points to each value, then the matrix would look like the next chart (X5/Y5). If you believe that government does have the right to ban certain activities for a driver with a cell phone (such as dialing the phone while the vehicle is in motion) but still allow others (such as receiving an inbound call), then this might illustrate your position.

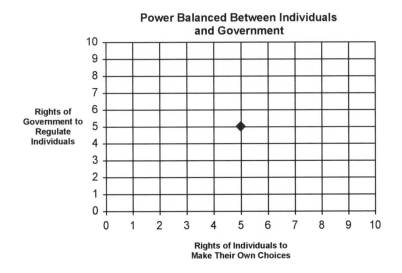

If you are someone who favors the Rights of Individuals over Rights of the Government, but still feel government needs to have some authority, then perhaps you would plot out as the next chart shows. If your position on the matrix is here (X7/Y3), then perhaps you think that all cell phone use in a vehicle is okay as long as the driver avoids continuously holding a phone to the driver's ear by using a hands-free device, thereby retaining the ability to steer.

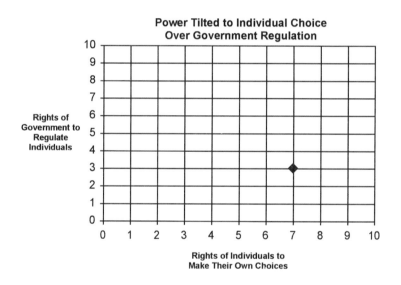

Looking at this chart may enable you to understand how political terminology is one of our greatest sources of conflict. Would you say that the political position shown here is a liberal one or conservative? If you say that liberalism is the resistance to control of individuals by the government, then isn't this position liberal? Or if you say that conservatism is the advocacy of the smallest government possible, then isn't this position conservative? Do you see how easily there can be two viewpoints to the exact same situation?

Isn't the more accurate response simply to say this person is someone who favors the Rights of Individuals over Rights of the Government, but still feels government needs to have some authority? Instead of asking people if they consider themselves to be liberal or conservative, wouldn't asking them where they would place themselves on this matrix be a more accurate reading of their political tendencies?

Also, depending on the topic, wouldn't you want to reserve the right to support a solution that was X2/Y8 just as easily as a position that was X8/Y2? Why then, do we (according to your particular definition of liberalism or conservatism) think that to be a true liberal you must always support a position left of X3/Y7? Or, conversely, why do we think that to be a true conservative you must always support a position right of X7/Y3?

Isn't stating your philosophy according to the matrix more flexible, more accurate and less contentious? Then how can we use this matrix in government policy? Let's explore that question.

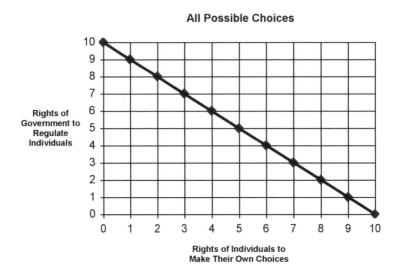

Overall, if you were to lay out all of the possible positions on the matrix, then the matrix would look as shown here.

Here is what all these charts should mean to you and how you can use them. If you can decide for yourself where you would position yourself on a matrix with two competing values, then isn't a political candidate or party able to do the same thing? What if you begin to use some objective criteria to determine if the candidate's and/or party's actions line up with what they say they believe?

Let's say we have political candidates or parties that say their governing principle (the rule of thumb they will apply to the issues they encounter) is to allow the greatest latitude possible in individual choice. What if they then take policy positions opposed to that on a purely personal matter? Isn't their position inconsistent at best and hypocritical at worst?

Let's consider a political party, for example, that says the party believes in the smallest government and the greatest personal freedom possible. What if that same party (which has received huge contributions from the auto insurance industry) then passes a law that bans all cell phone use by drivers of motor vehicles? Unless that party can show a truly compelling reason for this change, isn't their true governing principle their personal whims and self-interest? (Personal whims and self interest means politicians act to support the narrow views of the political base that funded their campaign, regardless of whether those views are destructive, irrational and just plain stupid. Even worse, politicians support the views of people who are, in essence or in actuality, bribing them.) If a politician is inconsistent, then isn't the politician untrustworthy? And if the politician is untrustworthy, then are you willing to re-elect that politician?

Perhaps the easiest way to understand consistency is this. Think of a politician you despise. Think of something that politician does that makes you furious. Now think of your favorite politician. Would your favorite politician still be your favorite if he or she was guilty of doing the same type of action as your hated politician? If so, then where is your consistency? Doesn't the old saying apply: "What's good for the goose is good for the gander?" Be honest now. Perhaps the worst lie you can tell is the one you tell yourself.

Ralph Waldo Emerson said, "What you do speaks so loud that I cannot hear what you say." A matrix like this can let you see clearly whether politicians' actions are consistent with what they say their values are.

Let's further develop this concept by helping you have what I call a "Holden Caulfield moment." I'll explain as we go forward.

A Holden Caulfield moment

Look again at the last figure – the matrix showing all the possible solutions X0/Y10 to x10/y0. Those positions are arrayed on a line that forms a hypotenuse on the right triangle of our 10-point matrix. What I'm going to do now is form a new chart using the hypotenuse as the horizontal, or x axis. With this new chart I want to show you why I contend **America is not nearly as polarized as it has been led to believe.**

Look at the next figure. What has been done here is to lay out the hypotenuse (all the possible positions from the last matrix, X0/Y10, X1/Y9, X2/Y8 and so on) along the bottom or horizontal axis.

My contention is this: Take 1,000 reasonably intelligent, open-minded people and an issue. Explain that issue to those people. Show all the points of view in a balanced way. Describe the possible solutions the same way a doctor might describe the possible methods of treatment for a major illness with the pluses and minuses clearly stated. Using normal statistical theory, the expectation would be that the majority of those 1,000 people would find one of those solutions more acceptable than the other. That position would usually be grouped around the X5/Y5 position on the horizontal axis. By plotting the number of people expected to take each possible position, a bar chart matrix is created. This matrix illustrates that probably

70 to 80 percent of the voters are grouped around a balanced X5/Y5 solution. And 10 to 15 percent of the voters (for a total of 20 to 30 percent) are grouped around an extreme position of either X1/Y9, or X9/Y1.

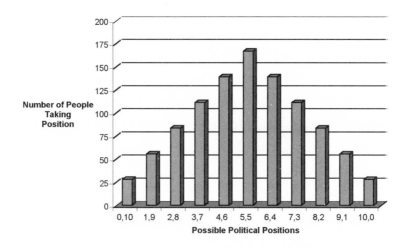

We are now very close to explaining what I mean by a "Holden Caulfield moment."

Look again at the matrix. Note how the bar over the X5/Y5 position is higher than all the others. The bar looks like a post that sticks up higher than all the others. What is being experienced in American politics is that the figurative political strategy of the extreme groups (those left of X2/Y8 and right of X8/Y2) is as follows. Both groups attempt to tie a conceptual rope to the "post" (those with an X5/Y5 orientation) and engage in a tug of war to pull at least 51 percent of the electorate to their view. They do so by disguising their actual orientation as a more moderate X4/Y6 or X6/Y4 position. But once you vote for them and you give them the power of elected office, these groups reveal themselves by constantly seeking to implement their extreme ideology.

Here is how the "Holden Caulfield moment" applies to all this. Holden Caulfield is the main character in the book *Catcher in the Rye*, by J.D. Salinger. Holden is a terribly confused and insecure teenager. He worries constantly about his own self worth and sufficiency in this world. Teenagers who read this book realize they are not the only teenagers in the world with these kinds of concerns. Teenagers think everyone else has their act together physically, mentally and emotionally, and they are the only one who has feelings of insecurity. Usually, teenagers are helped along with this misconception by a minority of their peers who attempt to shore up their own self-esteem by tearing others down. In fact, **every** teenager has these concerns. Holden is, therefore, normal, with lots and lots of company.

Here is how that applies to you as a citizen and a voter. Look again at the last figure. Note that 70 to 80 percent of you are grouped around the X5/Y5 position. Given an explanation of the circumstances, even people with a X7/Y3 or X3/Y7 position should be willing to compromise and agree with a more centrist position if they can be shown the logic in that position or promised some reasonable concession on another particular issue they are passionate about. So, **why are the 70 to 80 percent of us in the middle being held hostage by 20 to 30 percent of the ideological extreme?** Basically because we allow ourselves to be.

Two other points need to be made before summarizing

this chapter.

One of the sources of political conflict stems from the fact that some individuals or groups have something like an X1/Y9 or X9/Y1 position on an issue, but think their position is in the X4/Y6 to X6/Y4 range. Unless they can be persuaded as to their actual location on the spectrum, those individuals and groups will have to be dealt with as unreasoning zealots.

Sometimes the 70 to 80 percent grouping (depending on the nature of the issue) will be clustered around something like an X8/Y2 or X2/Y8 position. That's okay. If the group is exercising intelligence and common sense, then X8/Y2 and X2/Y8 positions will happen occasionally. Those who reject intelligence and common sense are those who insist that every issue has a solution left of X2/Y8 or right of X8/Y2. Such people have no credibility.

Realizing this, here is the message I wish to convey in my letter to the political parties.

For me to vote for you, I want to know that you embrace a political philosophy I can agree with. I recognize to win elections you must appeal to people who do not completely share my vision for what government should be and do. I am okay with that as long as the things you promise those other groups are in keeping with the following precepts. First, they offer solutions to problems **that serve the largest number of people for the longest period of time as balanced against doing the least harm or disruption to the least number of people and are the best solution monetarily we can get for the funds available among competing priorities.** Such solutions have minimal ripple effects and their impact on me physically, mentally/emotionally and financially is as small as possible.

If you tell me your philosophy is to favor the rights of individuals to make choices over the rights of government to regulate behavior (or vice versa), then be consistent with your philosophy in implementing policies. Don't run on one philosophy to be elected and then support legislation counter to that philosophy without substantial justification.

No matter who you are on this planet, no matter your nationality, your race, gender, age or status in society, you have one thing in common with everyone else. Each day lasts only 24 hours, and when that day is gone, the day will never come again. Our politicians should focus, therefore, on prioritizing the most critical tasks to be addressed first.

If you are prioritizing properly, then you will be governing on behalf of all the people, not just the extreme and vocal 20 percent with a narrow agenda. If you are doing intelligent things that seek abundance and tolerance for all, then those of us in the 80 percent will support you. If that means you must occasionally tell the 20 percent they may not have the things on their agenda that are not intelligent, curtail abundance for all or cause social intolerance, then we of the 80 percent will support you when you campaign for re-election.

☑

Five
Comparing Politics to Sailing and Boating

Analogy Four: Developing a Political Issue Position Is Like Sailing

The previous chapter showed you how to contend with groups that insist you have one of their monkey heads on your car. You were shown a consistent way to determine whether your beliefs would accept such a monkey head. This chapter will explore some of the ways mandatory monkey heads are allowed to become policy and how you can oppose those methods by becoming goal-oriented rather than issue-oriented. Let's use the analogy of sailing.

If you had a boat with a sail that could only be set for one direction, then you would be in trouble. A sailboat must have a sail that can be set to take advantage of whichever direction the wind blows. When you have a boat with a 360-degree sail, you are able to adjust the sail to go where you want. Remember, you cannot control the direction the wind blows. You can only control how you set the sail and how you hold the rudder in an attempt to harness the wind to go in the direction you want to go. Your destination doesn't change, but to get to your destination you must adjust how you set the sail and how you hold the rudder.

Clearly, there are parallels to this in issues our government confronts in an attempt to better us as a society and as a people. Just as the wind is uncontrollable, so, too, are the circumstances that confront us. The United States of America will always have enemies that wish the nation and its way of life ill. As much as we would wish people would not injure themselves doing foolish things, the fact remains people will injure themselves doing foolish things. Policies must be created, therefore, that are adaptable to the variety of unforeseen circumstances. That's because **the only certainty is the existence and occurrence of unforeseen circumstances.**

Having flexible policies means you are able to adjust the sail to continue to move toward the long-range policy position you want. As discussed in the last analogy, you are able to steer the ship of state toward the place that allows you to remain consistent with your goal of being fiscally responsible and socially tolerant. You don't want to allow political winds to blow you to a place where you are fiscally irresponsible and socially intolerant.

The key, whether you are sailing or setting political policy, is to know the destination you want before you set out on your journey. That's why knowing your values through the matrices you were just shown is so valuable to you. But now let's take that thought process another step further.

Let's say you wanted to go on a cruise to the Caribbean. You wouldn't select the cruise line based on whether it advertised itself as liberal or conservative would you? As the cruise was going on, how would you judge the performance of the ship's captain (and, therefore, the cruise line)? Wouldn't you ask yourself questions like these?

- Did the ship leave on time?
- Did the ship go to the ports advertised?
- Did the ship arrive at those ports on time as scheduled?
- Were you allowed sufficient touring time at each location?
- Did your accommodations meet your expectations?
- Did the food taste good?
- Was the entertainment satisfying?
- Were you allowed to choose between doing a lot and doing nothing?
- Was the sail as smooth as possible given the weather conditions on the water?

Look at that group of questions. Ask yourself these questions:

- As to performance, shouldn't our political leaders be judged according to the same sort of objective performance criteria for the issues they confront on behalf of the total population of the country?
- Shouldn't those solutions be defined by something other than whether the solutions are Democratic

or Republican, conservative or liberal?

- Shouldn't those solutions be judged by how well they work?

- Can't the goodness of a solution be judged by the answer to the following question? **Does this solution serve the largest number of people for the longest period of time as balanced against doing the least harm or disruption to the fewest number of people and is it the best solution monetarily we can get for the funds available among competing priorities?**

And isn't a major part of getting the right solution setting the proper goal? Or (restating the last sentence another way) isn't a major part of getting the right solution identifying the actual problem and developing a definition for the goal to meet with the solution? (More on this when politics is compared again to sports.)

Navigate the waters

Cruising right along by using another boating analogy, shouldn't finding solutions to our political issues be like setting buoys to a harbor entrance? The buoys marking the entrance are set to channel boats over the deepest part of the channel so that all boats can arrive at the dock without running aground. The buoys are **not** set to guide boats to a particular place in the harbor at the expense of other places in the harbor. The key issue to be determined in making the decision is where the deepest or lowest part of the land mass lies under the water. Now let's review this in a bit more detail and explore the parallels in political policy making.

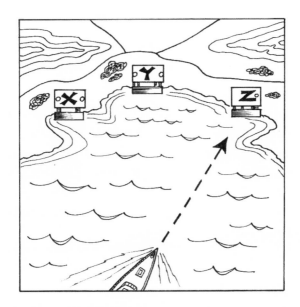

As this bird's-eye harbor view shows, from the water's surface you can see no obstructions to your path. You would choose the straightest line possible to take your boat from where you are to where you want to go in the harbor. Let's assume for the sake of illustration that you want to end up at the place marked Z on the right. Now look at the next drawing.

Taking the shortest distance between two points might run you aground on boulders beneath the water's surface. Clearly, markers are needed to keep boaters from doing this. So, one would presume that the rational approach would be to study and compare the depth of boat hulls using the harbor and the depth of the bottom of the harbor below the water's surface. With those data in hand, marker buoys can be set out as shown in the next illustration.

Here the buoys are optimally set to take advantage of the best the underwater terrain has to offer given the constraint of how deep the hulls of the boats are in the water. Note something else, because this lesson will come again and have use later. Certain options are shut off because they exceed the boundaries of smart behavior. If you have certain characteristics, then you might still be able to use those options, but those options do not fit the mold of doing the most good for the widest amount of people for the longest period of time and being the best financial solution among competing priorities. Now, what is meant by "options"? What if you are on a raft? If you're coming into the harbor on a raft, then you can probably go to the left of the left marker or the right of the right marker without running aground. If nobody is going to be hurt, then why shouldn't you be allowed to do that? Your raft is a monkey's head of your choosing, so who cares?

But what if you try to set the buoys to get everyone to buy rafts because you build rafts? That's another matter, isn't it?

Or what if we were to try to destroy the boulders so that the passage lane could be widened? Certainly that option is possible, but couldn't the money be better spent elsewhere on some other need, given the sufficiency of the solution based on the key issue of the depth of the hulls of the boats coming into the harbor versus the depth of the water in the harbor? The answer would seem to be yes, but then this becomes the point where an issue can become clouded and confused by politics.

Consider one other point about the placement of the buoys with relation to the underwater topography. What if the deepest part of the harbor wasn't exactly in the middle of the harbor entrance?

If you are consistent with your goal of providing the best solution, then the marker buoys would be placed according to the key factor of where the deepest part of the harbor entrance lies, regardless of whether the entrance is left, center or right. And this is where politics inserts itself in the process.

Usually, politics inserts itself in the following manner. Whoever owns the facility at location Z is not content with an approach to the harbor that gives an equal opportunity to their competitors at location X or Y. Z's owner uses influence to set the buoys to completely divert traffic to the right without regard to the depth of hulls.

Creating policy solely on the criteria of the ideology of self-interest may not work as well as a centrist policy of finding the key factors and writing the policy based on those key factors. Setting the markers to Z's benefit may put all boats moving toward Z, but not all boats may make it to Z. To complicate matters further, the owners of X may well be attempting to channel traffic to X and X alone.

So it is that the competition between the owners of X and Z (if they have their way) is keeping the boating public from enjoying the truly optimal solution.

Setting the buoys

How does this relate to real politics? Think of the elections you have experienced, particularly national elections. Don't the two major parties in the U.S. attempt to convince you that the way they want to set the buoys is the best way to set the buoys? Doesn't one party's policy seemingly attempt to force you ideologically to go to the left side of the harbor and the other force you to go to the right? Does either party advocate a balanced solution based on the true driving factors of the issues? Or do both parties base their policies on self-interest or ideology alone? Wouldn't you prefer that the policies be based on the true driving factors? That is to say (to repeat) **does this solution serve the largest number of people for the longest period of time as balanced against doing the least harm or disruption to the fewest number of people and is it the best solution monetarily we can get for the funds available among competing priorities?**

The key to having policies developed based on the true driving factors or key issues is to understand what the key issues are – that is, setting the buoys to mark the deepest area that will allow all traffic to pass without fear of running aground. The key issue is not to direct traffic to a destination to a chosen few to whom the politician is indebted. How do we know what the true driving factors are? We find out by asking good questions of ourselves.

The Bible says, "Ask, and it shall be given to you; seek and ye shall find. Knock and it shall be opened unto you" (New Testament, Matthew, vii, 7). Some interpret that passage to mean that if you ask God for a new car or some other improvement in your life, then God will provide it. Others contend the meaning of the passage is the better the questions you ask yourself, the better the data you get in your answers. The better the data from your answers, the better the solution will be for you.

Biblical scholars are not alone in this approach. If you read or listen to the works of many of the success mentors (people such as Tony Robbins, Jim Rohn or Stephen Covey, among others), you will find the same principles at work. What they teach is to reverse your "woe is me" thought process. Instead of asking yourself, "Why am I so poor?" ask yourself "How can I get more money?" Don't ask yourself questions about what you lack; ask yourself questions about what your possibilities are. Similarly, I hope you began reading this because you were asking yourself, "Why am I so frustrated by the current political structure?" and are gathering the data needed to ask yourself, "What do I need to do to have the political policies and activities I want?"

Adjust your course

If you as a voter want your elected representatives to make policy based on the crucial factors (the depth of the channel) and not self-interest (who owns property that will benefit from how the buoys are set), then two things must happen. First, demand that those you vote for set rules for themselves that will force them to give you the ethical, open and even-handed behavior you want. Second, define the goals you want to see achieved as a means of building toward consensus and make your representatives accountable to explaining how their actions work toward consensus. Let's discuss those two actions in more detail.

First, set the rules to get the behavior you want. The behavior you want of elected officials is to represent **all** their constituent voters and organizations with openness and fairness. Demand a level playing field for business, government and the general public. You don't have the time to keep up with all the issues that confront us. You need a press that acts as your watchdog to let you know when someone is abusing the public trust. To that end, demand and support a press that exposes betrayal of the public trust. Buy stock in the companies that own the major radio and TV broadcasting companies. As a stockholder, let the owners of those corporations know your support of their company and the products of their advertisers will depend on their service to you with watchdog activities. Demand that ownership of printing and broadcasting companies be dispersed, not consolidated. That is good not only for politics, but for the discovery and sustaining of a variety of new and talented artists and entertainers as well. You may also want to support the public financing of political campaigns so that politicians are not forced to prostitute themselves in order to gain financing for their campaigns.

Second (to paraphrase the writings of Stephen Covey), define your goals by beginning with the end in mind in stating what you want from government. These statements are why I say that it is possible to have a consensus on political issues that 70 to 80 percent of the population can agree on.

In determining solutions to our political issues, I fully acknowledge that most of those political issues do not have a fixed deep point that is easy to chart like the bottom of a sea harbor. As we journey toward the result we want, we will often be required to adjust our course. We would, therefore, do well to set a course with steering points that can tell us where we are in relation to where we want to go. Just like my compass example in the introduction, with three known points you can plot your location in a trackless desert with great accuracy. I think we as a nation can much more easily agree on where we are, where we want to go and the best course to take us there if we will keep in mind three basic principles about the government we want. **Those three principles are as follows: limited government, fiscal prudence and social tolerance.**

Think winter all summer

I want a limited government that provides fiscal prudence and social tolerance. Restated, I want a government that will be as limited in size and scope as it can be and as robust as it needs to be to do the job right the first time – that will be fiscally prudent and socially tolerant. Government is to individuals and institutions what mud is to log cabins. That is to say, if you think of a log cabin, think of how uncomfortable that cabin would be in the winter if there were nothing to block the space between the logs. Without the mud between the logs, there would be no way to trap the heat in the cabin and to keep the cold wind out of the cabin. In the same way, government acts with us as individuals and institutions (the logs that make up the cabin) to fill in the gaps and act in a way that makes our lives better.

I fear we have people who have lived in the cabin so long they have forgotten the benefits of the mud and want to do away with that mud. Those who feel that way will want to do so until an unwelcome wind like a Katrina blows through and shows how vulnerable we are individually and how strong we can be collectively.

The philosopher Jim Rohn says this about what he calls "the ant philosophy": "The ants think winter all summer." Human beings and their institutions would do well to copy this philosophy.

Since people can have different interpretations of words and phrases, allow me to further define some of the terms I'm using here.

By the term *limited government*, I mean a government that is as big as it has to be to do the needed job right the first time, but no bigger than it needs to be and that conducts its business legally within the confines of the Constitution.

Limiting the physical size of government (numbers of people, equipment and property) minimizes the tax dollars required to operate that government. Limiting the authority of government minimizes the intrusion of government into our personal lives.

I define *fiscal prudence* in government as a measure of those actions that raise sufficient funds for government's legitimate functions in order to avoid excessive debt and to meet its promised obligations now and in the future.

I define *social tolerance* in government as giving all faiths, creeds and other social groupings the opportunity to live and let live equally within the bounds of our Constitution.

So, when a search is under way for the solution to one of the many challenges we have, we can legitimately evaluate those proposed solutions by asking the following questions.

- What specific effects will a proposed solution have on people and their institutions?

- Will there be any negative ripple effects from allowing this policy?

- Is there a specific group of people already in existence and unable to defend themselves who will be severely harmed by this policy?

  Physically?
  Mentally/emotionally?
  Monetarily?

- Does implementing a solution set a precedent that opens the door to the creation of another policy that is unacceptable to a majority of Americans?

- Overall, does this solution serve the largest number of people for the longest period of time as balanced against doing the least harm or disruption to the fewest number of people and is it the best solution we can get monetarily for the funds available among competing priorities?

- Does this solution contribute to our goal of achieving simultaneously limited government, fiscal prudence and social tolerance?

We may ask other questions as well. Remember the cruise line questions we asked a few pages ago? What if you sat down and asked those same types of questions for yourself regarding the kind of government you want? Wouldn't you ask questions such as these:

- Does my government function in a way that makes real the ideals of the Declaration of Independence and the Preamble to the Constitution?*

- Does my government provide second-to-none security for this country and its citizens against enemies both foreign and domestic?

- Does my government take those economic, diplomatic and other measures needed to create allies instead of enemies and ensure that armed conflict is the last resort to ensure peace?

- Does my government take the required actions to ensure the social, cultural and religious freedom of behavior and expression for all its citizens?

• To read these documents again, check out **www.archives.gov**.

I have asked those questions – and more. As a result, I developed for myself a list of the requirements I think defines good government, particularly at the federal level.

Before reading this list, familiarize yourself with one other life lesson of mine. I was in the Army before night-vision devices were common. To prepare a defensive position for use during the night, I was taught to place stakes in the ground to the left and right of me based on where my fellow soldiers were. If I swung my rifle too far to the right or left to fire in the darkness, then I could be shooting at one of my own people. The stakes kept me from going too far to the left or right. Similarly, what you will see on my list are descriptions that can go to the left or right, based on the issue, but not exclusively to the left or the right, and neither too far to the left nor too far to the right.

My list:

What Do I Want from My Government?

Conduct the functions of the government in such a way the citizens of our country can continue to be free to do those things pleasing to them as they experience "life, liberty and the pursuit of happiness." Making government function this way means government must:

☑ Create and maintain military forces capable of defeating or deterring all current and potential enemies. This is our government's first and primary task, because if we lose a war to a foreign power, then we lose all freedom of choice in every other aspect of our lives. Those forces must be drawn from within the current population in such a way that the burdens of sustaining the force fall across all segments of the society. The methods used to create and maintain the force will incorporate checks and balances that forestall the abuse of power in the use of those forces. War must be fought in accordance with the time-honored and proven Principles of War in the most optimum way.

☑ Provide our country with the very best intelligence possible on the intentions and capabilities of our potential adversaries. Recognize that human intelligence is the best of all sources but requires the longest sustained effort to develop and must be consistently funded over the long term for best results.

☑ Supplement our military forces with diplomatic, economic and humanitarian organizations. Use those organizations to foster the best international relations possible and insure that the use of force is a little-used option of absolute last resort.

☑ Secure the existence of the citizens of this country in their own homes by

- Securing the borders of our country from harmful people and cargo.

- Maintaining sufficient law enforcement organizations to enforce existing laws against all forms of crime, including white-collar.

- Constantly reviewing and amending laws (unenforceable or of dubious value) that divert law enforcement from higher priorities.

- Securing commercial activities from vulner ability to terrorist activities.

- Ensuring a healthy food supply.

- Ensuring ongoing research providing new and better drugs that heal without unwanted consequences worse than the disease itself.

☑ Enact and enforce regulatory programs that recognize that profitable businesses are a boon to all members of society through the products they provide, the wages paid to workers and the tax revenue generated to support needed government activities. Seek at all times to level the playing field in business competition so that new businesses will have a chance to develop and consumers can have the best products possible. Provide oversight to ensure those products do not constitute a safety hazard or are offered at prices boosted by unfair conditions of monopoly. Ensure that the investments of individuals and organizations are protected from fraud.

☑ Enact and enforce programs that recognize businesses have a responsibility to treat workers well and to pay a living wage so their workers do not need or use government assistance programs. Maintain a balance in laws and regulations that enable business to dictate the unique internal adherence to process and procedures necessary to produce safe, desirable, and profitable products.

☑ Recognize the freedom of individuals to persuade others to adopt the precepts of their particular religion in their daily life as a personal choice. Guard against individuals attempting to use government to impose the adoption of the precepts of their particular religion on all citizens in the society.

☑ Minimize the expense of government by being forward thinking and applying Benjamin Franklin's age-old principle that an ounce of prevention is worth a pound of cure (think of the levees in New Orleans in 2005 as an example of this). Ensure that the ripple effects of an action are duly considered before that action is taken. At the same time, employ sufficient numbers of people in contingency planning for problems that people, plans and resources are in place to react to situations without unreasonable delay.

☑ Provide infrastructure (bridges, roads, dikes, levees, dams and the like) with forward-looking anticipation and prioritization of potential future events as a means of promoting commerce, enhancing the national defense and minimizing the impact of natural disasters.

☑ Use the power of government to shape behavior by its citizens to promote self-sufficiency for the country in natural resources and other areas. The first priority in this area is energy independence.

☑ Use the power of government to shape behavior by its citizens to promote environmental protection benefiting this generation and generations to come with clean air, soil and water. Resist the temptation to put the stamp of mankind on the last vestiges of unspoiled wilderness for the sake of temporary monetary profit. Maintain some portions of the planet within our boundaries so future generations may know our earth as it was in our earliest days as a nation.

☑ Collect the revenue needed for governmental programs in a way that promotes tight-fisted fiscal soundness with minimal inflation. Avoid the accumulation of excessive debt, particularly to foreign countries in order to avoid the undesirable influence those countries might attempt to apply and thereby restrict us from acting in our own self-interest. Collect taxes equitably across society. Let no source of wealth or income be exempt from taxes in a way that unfairly benefits one segment of the society at the expense of another segment. Constantly seek to simplify and equalize the way people and institutions are taxed.

☑ Provide an affordable health care system that balances the profit motive for health care providers with the right of citizens to have health care. Provide incentives and training that channel individual citizens to toward taking personal responsibility for maintaining their health.

☑ Provide educational opportunity for all members of our society. Do so in a way that recognizes that those who fail to develop basic skills at an early age are much more likely to be a liability to society. Providing adequate resources in a timely manner creates students who become productive citizens, supporting families, paying taxes, voting intelligently and providing for their own long-term security. They are less likely to be a burden to society, requiring tax dollars to account for their existence in support systems or the legal system (courts and prison). At the same time, individuals must be confronted with and made to understand the personal responsibility and necessity of learning as surely as they are taught reading and writing. Teachers have a responsibility to teach, but students have an equal responsibility to learn. Those students not only uninterested in their own education, but also disruptive to the learning process for others must be dealt with swiftly and not permitted to disrupt those who are diligent about their education. Although parental authority is the first line of defense in this area, government must provide the tools necessary to make this possible when parental authority is inadequate. Providing resources necessary to ensure that basic lessons are being grasped at the appropriate age, therefore, is essential to the overall long-term health of the country.

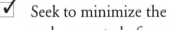 Seek to minimize the number of people in prison and executed for crimes. Maintaining high

numbers of people in prison who do not represent a significant threat to society provides a drain on resources needed elsewhere. Studies show that the execution of prisoners is actually more expensive to society than life imprisonment. Still, some crimes are so heinous and revolting that extreme punishments are justified. In those cases, society should not shrink from exacting the ultimate payment from those who have violated that society. Ensure that adequate prison capacity exists to the point that no prisoner with a high potential for damage to society is released due to crowding or capacity issues.

☑ Everyone applauds those fortunate enough to win a significant prize from the various lotteries around the country. Simultaneously, our citizenry must recognize that some members of society are the victims of a negative lottery. Those members struck by the negative lottery have contacted debilitating diseases, been the victims of an accident, or suffered some other incidents (particularly if these happen before someone is able to accumulate the resources or insurance products to provide for themselves). Members of a caring society recognize there but for the Grace of God, there they go themselves. That society instructs its government to institute and maintain programs for the benefit of such people. Such programs seek not just to care for those in those circumstances, but to eliminate the causes of the circumstances and to find ways to restore those individuals as functioning members of society. Simultaneously guard against designing programs in such a way that those who are too lazy to work and those whose main industry is to exploit the role of victim they have undeservedly given to themselves can cheat the American taxpayer.

☑ Speaking again of the lottery, let government enact tort legislation to ensure that individual businesses are not vulnerable to being played like a slot machine in an attempt by individual citizens to get rich quick through our court systems. Simultaneously, business should not be allowed to short-cut research and development or operational procedures in identifying and preventing product defects (even when the legal system sets affordable caps on damages paid in lawsuits).

☑ (The following may seem like a given, but recent events make its enunciation necessary.) Let those who create, administer and adjudicate our laws do so within the boundaries of the Constitution and the Bill of Rights. Let changes to the Constitution be made slowly, with the greatest care and concern for all who are affected by the changes. The conduct of those with elected and appointed office must be above reproach with regard to honesty and clearly demonstrate the consideration of fairness to all elements of society and without taking advantage of their position for personal gain.

What's on your list?

This is my list. You may have other points to add or points you would amend. Note the balance in the approach. My list recognizes there are two points of view to be reconciled. Contrast that with the rhetoric you will often see from the two major parties. Note their frequent use of one-sided hyperbole (the "magnet" described earlier).

You can use this list to judge the effectiveness of government in the following manner. Phrase the policy goals listed here as questions. For example, "Is government providing educational opportunity for all members of our society? Is government doing so in a way that recognizes that those who fail to develop basic skills at an early age are much more likely to be a liability to society?"

Goals enable us to be goal-oriented instead of issue oriented in the face of unrelenting 24/7/365 news coverage. Here's how the benefit comes.

How do you know you are in the presence of a talented stand-up comedian? You know because the comedian has an impeccable sense of timing. The comedian gets you to laugh at something. Just before you stop laughing, the comedian hits you with another punch line, and you laugh again and again until you can't stop laughing.

Those in the news business operate on the same principle. They have ratings to preserve and advertising to sell, so they must keep your attention every day with new attention-getting issues. These issues are like a wind that constantly shifts direction while you are sailing. If you don't have goals, then you can easily be blown around by those shifting winds. When you have goals, you merely adjust the set of the sail and the way you hold the rudder, thus enabling you to continue on to the goal you had in the first place. Your goal does not change, only your way of reaching your goal changes. (Check the cartoon on the next page to see a funny depiction of this concept.)

If you agree with having policy goals as an approach, then you may now ask yourself:

"Why can't I get that approach?" and

"What is being done to divert us from that approach?"

The answer to the first question is found in the previous chapters. You can't get that approach because the political parties have found another way to victory. That way is to distract us with blood-pressure-raising emotional monkey-head issues. The issues divide us, enabling the parties to use a strategy that gives them control with just over 50 percent of the vote and then lets them do what they like once they are in office.

To address the second question, let's return to the analogies comparing politics to sports, but before we return to the analogies, let's quickly summarize this chapter.

Bob Gorrell, Creators Syndicate, Inc., www.gorrellart.com

I want a government that sets policies that are flexible for the inevitability of changing circumstances. At the same time, the changes that are made must enable the government to remain consistent toward its philosophy.

I want to see government use a philosophy that **seeks those solutions that serve the largest number of people for the longest period of time as balanced against doing the least harm or disruption to the fewest number of people and are the best solutions monetarily we can get for the funds available among competing priorities.**

Further, that government will seek solutions to take us from our focus on issues to a focus on goals that **contribute to our overall goal of simultaneously achieving limited government, fiscal prudence and social tolerance.**

Finally, the solutions we seek will be based on trying to find the equivalent of the deepest part of the harbor to set the buoys and not trying to steer the harbor traffic toward the largest political donor.

✓

Six
Comparing Sports to Equal Opportunity, Foreign Policy and Media Influence

Analogy One (Continued): How Your Relationship to Politics Is Like Your Relationship to Sports

Let's return to comparing politics to sports. In our first chapter on this topic, we considered three questions.

- Is politics like a sport you don't like? If so, what are the impacts you need to consider?

- Or is politics like a sport you like, but for which you don'thave time?

- Or is politics like a sport you like, but don't understand?

Having covered that aspect of the comparison, three other comparisons of sports and politics will now be discussed. Perhaps our common understanding of sports will ease our understanding of politics, make discussing political topics easier and help us to understand how our political commentators may be hindering us in being goal oriented in getting the government performance we want. The three comparisons are these:

- Are there parallels between sports and political topics such as equal opportunity?

- Are there parallels between sports and our foreign policy?

- Are there parallels between the statistical detail sports fans possess and the statistics voters should demand to be applied to political policies and functions?

Are there parallels between sports and political topics and programs such as equal opportunity and welfare?

A coach has a responsibility to play the best players possible based on ability. The coach should not decide which players will play because of their family connections. Players should expect to be chosen based on their skill and potential. They should not expect special dispensation because of personal characteristics such as race and gender or because of the social/economic position of a player's parent. To do otherwise is a betrayal of the community that supports the team and wishes the best team possible to compete as its representative.

Similarly, we as citizens have an expectation that our government's elected leaders will fill key positions with people selected because they are qualified to perform in those positions. People should not be selected as a reward for service to a political party when those people lack the qualifications to perform in their assignment.

Because of these same principles, citizens need to expect their government to proclaim and enforce another message: The rules for competition are the same for everyone. Do not expect the rules of the game to change to accommodate you exclusively at the expense of someone else. How ludicrous would it be: a 10-foot-high-regulation-basketball goal for the home team and an 11-feet-high goal for the visiting team! What makes sport such viable entertainment all over the world is that competition is conducted under rules that are the same and fair for all the players. The drama becomes how well the players can perform in direct competition on a level playing field. The attraction of that drama sells many a ticket to all types of events around the world. As a result, countless young men and women devote hour after hour to the development of the skills required to compete on the largest stages possible for the potential of the lucrative paydays those stages represent. Those men and women know there will be no golf or bowling-like governmental handicap to add to their score to help them compete. They know that they will win or lose solely on how high their mind and body will allow them to perform.

Why, then, is our educational system seemingly unable to impress upon segments of American youth what the rules and skills are that lead to economic success? What unconventional approaches are needed to convince youth that:

- The only thing unchanging about the world they face is continuous change?
- The basic skills of reading, mathematics and science are essential to success?

- Overcoming peer pressure to be mediocre must be resisted?

- Discipline and adherence to a strong work ethic pays off in the long run?

If our society through our government provides every opportunity to learn and to prepare for a life of satisfying work and prosperity, then that society owes no debt to those students who refuse to take advantage of those opportunities. That is a message that deserves to be communicated early and often throughout the period of time an individual is a student.

Simultaneously, part of the preparation society should provide (in contrast to the years before the global economy) is an orientation towards entrepreneurship and independence, not just employment working for someone. To that end, practical courses in money management, business ownership, sales, negotiation, statistics and other similar subjects should be part of the curriculum. In addition, let us combat obesity and ill health by making fitness programs part of the student's day once again and possibly adding physical fitness testing to graduation requirements.

There are at least two other things I think society should provide I will discuss here. One is that society needs to acknowledge the time children need to spend in school must expand. Knowledge expands year after year, but the time that teachers have to teach has not expanded since our days as an agrarian society. This is a very complex topic which cannot be fully explored here. I feel it important enough, however, to draw attention to it.

The other thing I wish to mention is the fact we could do much to improve academic performance in our society were we to fully address the mental, emotional and physical abuse of children commonly called bullying. For more on this topic, I invite the reader to review the content at **www.bullysafeusa.com** and to read the books and other resources offered there. Children who worry about being bullied are not children who can wholly focus on academic achievement.

Are there parallels between sports and our foreign policy?

There are several parallels between sports and our foreign policy, which can contribute to our understanding of the kind of government we want for ourselves.

Inter-collegiate sports in America are controlled by the National Collegiate Athletic Association (NCAA). The member colleges and universities adhere to the rules and regulations of the NCAA. Those rules and regulations are designed to ensure that no single institution gains an unfair advantage over its competitors, either on or off the field. Consequently, NCAA rules cover not only the rules of the games themselves, but also topics such as practice time, recruiting restrictions and payments to players. All of these are designed to ensure that a college or university is not able to use the wealth of its alumni to dominate a particular sport year after year.

Although this approach might be appropriate for athletics, it is totally inappropriate as a policy for our national defense. In national defense, America must be the continuous and perennial champion of champions. We must have a team that is so good that the other teams forfeit games to us by default rather than endure the pain of competing. This is what is known as deterrence. If the day ever comes that America loses its ability to defend its way of life, then our way of life is gone. Not only will books like this one not matter, but all the things we debate will also fall by the wayside because there will be no debate allowed. In those circumstances, getting our way of life back will require a price in blood and treasure many times the cost of keeping it in the first place.

Some say we have no need for military defense. Do we have no need for police? Think of it this way. Level of ambition in commerce is dependent on personal ambition and capability. Some are content with a mom and pop operation. Others wish to create a national network of businesses. Still others have a vision of international commerce. The same level of ambition in commerce applies to war. War is only crime on a larger scale. Some criminals steal wheel covers. Some criminals steal retirement accounts and convert business and government funds to personal use. Some criminals steal whole countries and their people. Our military forces and intelligence services provide the shield. Behind the shield, our country is able to generate the wealth and way of life that for so long has been the envy of the world.

Still, we have need for checks and balances in the creation and use of our Armed Forces. How do we keep the forces from being used to bully other nations or ostensibly rescue us from a threat that turns out not to be real? While there will always be a need to replace aging equipment and to maintain our winning edge with technological advantages in new equipment, how much is enough? At what point are we putting too much money into military hardware at the expense of domestic needs? Further, are we putting too much emphasis on equipment, ignoring the fact that wars are fought and won by people?

Part of the fairness in sports is having an even number of players on both teams, but not in war. If you have the capacity to play 16 on 8, or 24 on 8, you do it (hockey being a good example of an exception; if a player is sent to the penalty box, the teammates must play short-handed). If we are forced to fight a war, then we don't seek to be fair in terms of numbers of combatants or technological advantage. We seek to win because winning is vital. One of the keys to the success of offense is amassing superiority in numbers at the point of attack. If we as a nation are unwilling to commit the forces necessary to win, then we should not go to war. If we are unwilling to commit the forces necessary and we do go to war, then if we fail (and we will likely fail), all we have done is reveal that we are unwilling to pay the price to win. And if we do that, then we encourage our enemies to persist and expand against us.

General Douglas MacArthur was quoted as saying, "In war, there is no substitute for victory." In the world of commerce, the former head of General Electric, Jack Welch, had a self-imposed rule for business. Welch said, "If you don't have a competitive advantage, don't compete."

Switching metaphors, I want to recall a scene from the movie *The Untouchables*. In this scene, the grizzled Irish cop played by Sean Connery is trying to advise the young and idealistic Elliot Ness (portrayed by Kevin Costner) on what it will take to bring down the mobster empire of Al Capone. Connery says something to the effect, "If they come at you with a knife, you pull out a gun. If they send one of yours to the hospital, you send two of theirs to the morgue." Costner's character wavers to make the necessary commitment. Not until after Connery's character is gunned down does Costner as Ness understand that evil must be confronted by any means possible. Why? Because evil, like a poisonous snake or a shark, will just keep coming until it is either locked away or destroyed.

We have little difficulty in getting the best and most talented of our youth to participate in sports. The potential for fame and financial reward provides all the incentive necessary. Now consider this. What if that potential for fame and financial reward were taken away and leaving only the risk of pain, injury, dismemberment or death? How difficult would it be to get young men to play football, for example, if the sport offered no reward, only risk? What if community spirit and self-esteem revolved around the success or failure of the high school's football team? What if, despite the potential loss of community well being, the biggest, fastest, strongest and smartest athletes refused to play?

Even worse, what if the stakes for the game results were not just self-esteem but the community's freedom and economic prosperity? What if, even in light of these vital stakes, our young people refused to play? Even worse yet, what if the wealthy parents of big, fast, strong and smart athletes refused to let their children play? In other words, it's okay to let other people's children risk pain, injury, dismemberment or death on behalf of the community's well being, but not their own children. Could it be that one of the reasons that some parents refuse to let their children participate is that they believe that freedom and prosperity are not truly at risk?

World War II has such a good and strong memory in the minds of Americans because victory was earned as a community effort. All levels of American society participated in that conflict, including two sons of the late Ambassador Joseph Kennedy (one of the two died and the other became President of the United States), the grandson of President Teddy Roosevelt, and the son of former Senator Prescott Bush, who was a decorated Navy pilot and became the 41st President of the United States, George H.W. Bush.

Understand this dynamic about our country today. We do not have a volunteer military. We have a **recruited** military based on financial incentives. How do we know if pursuing a war is in the national interest and if the total costs of that conflict have been considered before entering it, if only our volunteers/recruits are at risk for pain, injury, dismemberment or death? This topic will be discussed in more depth in a later chapter.

One other aspect of comparing sports to foreign policy is worth mentioning. Actually, this point can apply to either foreign or domestic policy, but this is as good a place as any to discuss that aspect. What is worthy of mention here is the impact of radio and television commentators on your perception of how the contest is being played. This aligns somewhat with what we have already discussed in the section on matrices and self interest.

One year I was watching a playoff game for the National Football League (NFL). The defending champion team was losing. The "color" commentator (that is, the ex-jock expert in the sport who tells you about the strategy of each of the two teams – not only what just happened, but why it happened) was providing his analysis. The commentator talked about why the defending champion was losing, not why the challenging team was winning. That approach was probably justified, because the champions were not performing to their usual standards. They had made several errors, such as losing the ball several times and giving the challengers extra opportunities to score. Had it not been for those errors, the game would have been much closer.

I didn't care who won, so when I reflected on those comments later, I saw no bias in the comments. Had I been for the challenger team, I certainly might have taken offense that the color commentator was not primarily attributing the success of the challenger to the challenging team's skill and playing attributes.

Allow me to provide you one other example, and then I'll tell you why I'm providing it.

I am a long-time fan of one of the NFL teams. Once in a

while, when I'm watching one of their games on television, I will turn down the sound on my television and listen to the team's radio broadcast. Listening to a radio broadcast by the team's broadcast crew is much different than experiencing a television broadcast. Beyond the obvious lack of a visual signal, the difference is the deliberate detachment of the television announcers in order to give a balanced view of the contest without favoring one contestant or the other.

Such is not the case on the radio. In my case, my team's color commentator was a former quarterback for the team. He's now in the NFL Hall of Fame. There is no doubt in the mind of the listeners that he as well as the other members of the radio broadcast crew want "our" team to win. It's interesting because, despite the blatant us-versus-them orientation, the former quarterback will not shrink from criticizing the team – his team. If things are not going well, then the listener is told why play is not going well and what needs to be done to turn things around. And if the other team (who is there to win as well) makes a good play with its intellect and athleticism, then our former quarterback commentator is quick to give praise to a worthy opponent.

Considering this, here's my question: **Are the talking heads on political programs as neutral as they should be?** Do the obvious partisan critics criticize their team when it makes obvious errors, or do they always find some means of trying to "spin" an event into a positive for the side they favor? Do they applaud or endorse when the side they generally oppose has an achievement or a proposal that is good for the country as a whole? Or do they criticize that achievement or proposal simply because their side was not the author?

If the answers to these questions is no, then their reporting lacks credibility, fairness and balance. I, for one, distrust such reporting, and I hope you will learn to distrust it too. Clearly, this is another example of principle centered versus self-interest-centered politics.

Here is another sports example for you to consider. Why do we applaud the ability of a coach to make adjustments to players and to the coach's scheme during a contest to turn defeat into victory, yet assail politicians who change their position on a topic because of improved information regarding that topic? To me, the politicians who deserve a derisive tag like "flip flopper" are the ones who practice self-interest-centered politics and refuse to change their positions on an issue when additional information clearly indicates that the change gives the country a solution that serves the largest number of people for the longest period of time as balanced against doing the least harm or disruption to the fewest number of people and it is the best solution monetarily we can get for the funds available among competing priorities.

One other aspect of journalistic criticism is worth noting. Would you say that my team's Hall of Fame quarterback should not make his comments during the game? After all, why can't the opposing team listen to the broadcast and use that information to its advantage? If you think that, my reply would be simple. That's garbage. The other team already knows what your team's weaknesses are and is already at work trying to exploit them. Acknowledging the blatantly obvious to the competent is not disloyalty.

Clearly, in war (as in sports) there is a consideration of operational security for your side's activities. No team's fans would be in favor of having a camera or microphone inside a huddle describing precisely what their team was going to do next and broadcasting such data in a way that the opposing team could act directly on that data. Similarly, revealing data about military operations in a way that exposes our people and the success of the operation to death and failure is criminal.

The balancing view is that the people in a representative government deserve to know when their elected leaders are not performing their duties in a way that will lead to victory. Wouldn't revealing poor military planning energize improvement in planning, lead to success and save lives? Wouldn't that be patriotic?

Are there parallels between the statistical detail sports fans possess and the statistical reality voters should demand to be applied to political policies and functions?

One of the phenomena of American society, particularly in the larger cities where the major professional sporting teams reside, is the popularity of talk radio and sports talk shows. These shows provide the opportunity for fans to share their opinions about what is wrong or right with their favorite team. These fans can be zealots, and they study and understand their team and its sport in not only the competitive on-the-field aspect, but (in the case of professional sports) the business aspects, as well.

Let's make up a story here to illustrate a point. (I apologize that I'm about to use an example for a sport that is a bit technical. While I think the point of the story will still be understandable, I invite anyone who doubts the basis for the example to check its veracity with someone who understands this aspect of football.)

Let's assume we're talking about a professional football team that ranks 30 out of 32 in the league in run defense. To improve this statistic, the coach is proposing to place all 11 defending players on the line of scrimmage. Such a proposal would generate screams of protest. Why? Because the fans of the team may be for the team and want the team to win, but they refuse to endorse stupidity on the part of the team's leadership. The knowledgeable fans understand that the lack of depth in this type of defense has at least two major weaknesses that would be exploited by decent teams.

No knowledgeable fan would fall for a variation on this theme. Let's say that a team is ranked 30 out of 32 in run defense and 2 out of 32 in pass defense. Would the knowledgeable fan accept the team's excuse that run defense is not important and look how well the team is doing in pass defense? No, the knowledgeable fan recognizes that the reason the passing defense number looks so good is that opposing teams have no need to pass to win.

How do we relate these examples to the political parties?

First, just as you may have made yourself into a knowledgeable sports fan, make yourself into a knowledgeable voter. As stated earlier, as much as you may love the sport you love, whoever wins the championship will not usually affect how you are allowed to live, what you're taxed on, and how much you pay in taxes. Therefore, it is up to you to learn at least the fundamentals about things like economics and tax policy. It is up to you to be able to recognize when some politician is (as Judge Judy says) peeing on your leg and telling you it's raining.

Where do you get this knowledge? You get it from reading and asking questions. This is not the kind of knowledge you get from sound bites on the radio and television. You say you don't like to read? Then accept the fact that you are doomed to being manipulated for the rest of your life. I hope I'm preaching to the choir here. You are, after all, reading this book. But others may have to be reminded of Mark Twain's quote on the subject. Twain wrote, "Those who will not read have no advantage over those who cannot."

With regard to taxation and spending, let me recommend some bipartisan and independent sources:

- Concord Coalition (**www.concordcoalition.org**: As they say on their Web site, "The Concord Coalition is a nonpartisan grassroots organization dedicated to informing the public about the need for (sic) generationally responsible fiscal policy." Recall that one of the steering marks I have for the government I want is fiscal responsibility. The Concord Coalition will give you the data you need to tell the difference between fiscal responsibility and fiscal irresponsibility.

• *Perfectly Legal*, a book by David Cay Johnston: The book shows (to quote its jacket), "Whether your family makes $30,000 or $300,000 a year, you are being robbed because the Internal Revenue Service (IRS) and other institutions have been systematically corrupted – under both Republican and Democratic administrations – to serve the needs of people who make millions." Not only does the book show how we have arrived in our current state, it also shows the flaws in current proposals that would only make things worse. Finally, the book makes proposals you may well want to endorse to your elected representatives.

• Kindred Minds Enterprises (**www.KindredMindsEnt.com**): If you are interested in other sources contributing to your understanding of politics and related subjects, please see our Web site. Use the "Contact Us" feature if you have a specific question. The reality, however, is that none of us has the time (and perhaps the intellect) to be able to understand all the highly technical subjects our legislators must deal with. Consequently, the best we can do is to elect the smartest people we can and require them to subject themselves to the highest standards of ethical conduct.

Part I: Summary

Where Are We, and Where Are We Going?

In terms of my own political philosophy, this is what I have presented so far.

You should be interested in politics. Politics affects you personally. Politics affects how you're allowed to live, what you're taxed for and on and how much you're taxed. Every dollar you're taxed is a dollar diverted from your own personal goals, desires and ambitions.

In essence, you are being manipulated by both parties. Both parties use monkey-head issues to manipulate you both positively and negatively. Some monkey heads are optional without side effects to you personally and are, therefore, acceptable. Others are not optional, and you have been given a way to tell the difference.

You have been shown how both parties implement their strategy for control using monkey-head issues. The parties are able to do this because they keep you issue oriented instead of goal focused based on your political values and philosophy. These strategies are designed to give a zealous minority political control to pursue a narrow agenda rather than governing for the greater good through a consensus.

You have been instructed in a means to discover for yourself your personal political values and philosophies.

Knowing your personal political values and philosophies, you were presented with a method to determine whether a policy is being proposed based on values you support or on the self-interest of the politicians and the interest groups they favor. You were also shown how to decide whether a party's policies were consistent or inconsistent with the values the party supposedly represents, as well as with your own personal values.

You were given an example of how to convert your orientation from an easily manipulated issue orientation to a solid broad-based goal orientation with easily visible steering principles for you to evaluate whether a proposed policy is moving toward or away from the goals you have as a citizen.

You have been provided with an even-handed methodology for thinking about political topics to move you away from the confrontational language of the talking heads on the political shows to a language of consensus.

You have been shown through a statistical model how the adoption of the centrist philosophy is likely shared by the vast majority of voters. If those voters communicate that philosophy to the two political parties, then the conflicting philosophies of the Extreme Right and the Extreme Left might be cast aside to create a new majority. That new majority has the potential to move America forward to new heights of intelligence, abundant achievement and tolerance.

You have been offered a variety of action steps you can take as an individual to have a positive impact in making this philosophy a reality.

In Part Two, you will see the application of the philosophy and its reasoning to some of the major issues of our times.

These are the issues on a level with prohibition keeping us from moving forward because they are not resolved, just revisited. We continue to be manipulated and distracted by these issues. Until we reach a consensus as a nation and put these issues behind us, we truly will be unable to use our limited time to pursue the higher priorities of peace, prosperity and abundance we deserve.

In Part Three, you will be shown additional steps you can take if you are in agreement with this book's philosophy and want to put the principles into practice to guide the government that represents you. You must let the elected representatives and their parties who make up that government know that this is what you want so they will have the confidence to reject the radical wants of the Extreme Right and the Extreme Left.

Part II
Seeing Through the Smokescreens

An Introduction to the Issues

Caution to readers: Although I recognize it is the practice and prerogative of people to read ahead in a book, I urge you not to do so. If you read ahead at this point, you are doing so without the skills and perspective the earlier parts of this book give you. You'll be missing the background needed to fully appreciate the points being made.

Beware of one other pitfall, even if you have read Part One. Don't presume that because the way one issue is analyzed produces a conclusion you don't agree with that you won't agree with other issues. In fact, if there is an objective reason you think the conclusion should be different, then go to the Web site and tell me what you think that reason is. I may be wrong. I often am.

The topics in Part Two keep us in constant turmoil. Preoccupation with those issues provides a smokescreen. Actions are taken behind that smokescreen. And some of them may not be in our long-term self-interest economically, security-wise, or socially. Meanwhile, issues affecting our long-term interest economically, security-wise, or socially are not acted upon.

Regardless of who we are on this planet, we all get 24 hours every day. And every day that we continue to be distracted by smokescreen issues is a day that more pressing problems grow bigger to the point of crisis and beyond. We need to settle the smokescreen issues and move on. When the smokescreen issues are neutralized, 25 to 30 percent of the population will throw a temper tantrum and predict doom and gloom. The rest of us will go about our business and enjoy this life.

I am offering issues in play since forever. They have never been resolved. They are the 600-pound gorillas, the sacred cows of American politics. We have always had these kinds of issues. We have resolved slavery, prohibition and voting rights. Now it's time to solve the rest.

There are a great many candidates for analysis. Let me describe several, and then pick a few for an in-depth look.

National Defense and Homeland Security

How should we choose who fights for us? How should we determine the size and nature of our defense force? How do we determine what equipment that defense force needs? Remember that war is crime on a larger scale. We would not abolish police departments. We cannot abolish our military. How do we integrate homeland security into the national defense equation? How do we decide which conflicts are worth fighting and which are not? How do we balance our desire for security with maintenance of our rights as citizens of this country? This will be one of the topics explored in depth.

Taxation and Its Impact on Fiscal Sanity

I have noted that government is the mud in the cracks of a governmental log cabin. That mud must be purchased through taxation. Because that mud, like oxygen, has always been there, those who criticize taxes fail to see where we would be without that mud. They fail to see that taxes create a haven that shelters us from the ravages of many types of storms. Without that haven, we would doubtless find life much more difficult than it already is.

My philosophy is that I want taxes to support Benjamin Franklin's admonition that an ounce of prevention is worth a pound of cure. Would you rather pay for the creation of a functioning human being or for the incarceration of a dysfunctional human being? Which vital government function do you want shut down? Which road not paved? Which prison closed? Which security activity done away with? Do you want to take turns on sentry duty every night in your house or do you want to be able to rely on police being on patrol and a fire department you can call? Are calls for revisions to the tax code such as the Fair Tax proposal truly beneficial to the majority of taxpayers or merely another smokescreen to enable those with money to take advantage of others less fortunate?

Matters of Sexual Behavior and Personal Choice

Think of stores such as Wal-Mart, Target, K-Mart, Sears, and JC Penney. You probably prefer one store on that list and dislike another. Think of the one you dislike. What if that store engaged in political activism to get a law passed that everyone must shop at that store? You would be outraged, wouldn't you? The activities of some religious groups are like the store you don't like engaging in political activism to get a law passed that everyone must shop at that store. Some religious groups are tired of trying to convince you to adopt the beliefs of their religion. They hope, by taking control of the political process, to legislate and therefore impose/mandate their religious beliefs on you. They have gotten tired of their message being rejected and want to force you to adopt it, like it or not, with enforcement by governmental police and courts. The two primary issues in this category that cause us so much grief are abortion and gay marriage. Others, such as euthanasia and stem cell research, loom on the horizon.

Could the blurring of the line between church and state create a trend that will eventually lead to some sort of religious litmus test in order for the unfortunate to receive government aid? Are the requirements of some religious groups for political action accounting for the ripple effect of implementing those requirements? The freedom **of** religion guaranteed by the Constitution carries with it freedom **from** religion. How do we find the balance between incorporating the best features of religion and still allowing individuals to make their own choices in how they want to live their lives?

Illegal Drugs and Alcohol

Are we actually facilitating illegal drug pushers by making alcohol unavailable to 18- to 20-year-olds? Why is it that at 18 you are old enough as a soldier to look through the sight of a weapon and kill another human being, but you are not old enough to walk into a bar and order a beer? Why is a 19-year-old tried as an adult for underage drinking? If a 19-year-old is an adult, shouldn't they be allowed to drink?

I recall one of the original episodes of the television show *Dragnet*. The hero, Joe Friday, and his partner are staking out a candy store because candy stores have been robbed lately. Friday's partner is talking about workers in a candy store. The partner says that when workers are hired they are told they can have all they want. The first few days the workers eat a lot. After the first few days the workers are sick of the candy and eat hardly any at all. Could a similar adult-supervised approach to alcohol have similar results? Realize the reality: Because 18-year-olds can't buy alcohol in a bar by the drink, they buy under the table in bulk and drink in bulk. Are there other more common-sense approaches that could reduce the forbidden fruit mystery and allure of alcohol and other drugs? I think there are.

I realize the concern about binge drinking by young people. Current policies are only encouraging binge drinking. My proposals will discourage binge drinking. By legalizing drinking of 18-20 year olds, those youngsters will be more likely to drink where adult responsible supervision is present. At present they drink in secluded locations without this benefit. We should enable parents to be instructive with their children in the same way they instruct about driving a car, handling a firearm or sexual activity.

With regard to illegal drugs, the application of economic theory is very tempting to think about. According to economic theory, if there were no demand, then there would be no supply, because there would be no profit to be made. That being true, why are we not attacking the demand side more so than trying to restrict the supply of illegal drugs? If we were to allow the sale of drugs such as heroin or cocaine in 40-pound bags (like the horse crap it really is) then wouldn't the people who use it overdose and die sooner? Wouldn't this then rid society of those who want this product and wouldn't the example of their deaths drive demand down to its lowest possible ebb? Couldn't we tax drugs in the bargain and collect money from the fools who use illegal drugs instead of spending tax money to keep them apart from it?

These are contrarian views, I know, that would require thorough examination and the ability to account for unintended consequences. I make those thoughts known as someone who has in his memorabilia an underground newspaper in which he is featured as an evil being for his skill at apprehending people using illegal drugs. But aren't these concepts worthy of further examination?

Rich People Versus Poor People

As you read various political books and Web sites in this part of the 21st century, you often encounter two adversarial points of view. One view is that poor people are poor because they are lazy. Those who hold this view feel that the poor are detracting from the rich's ability to hold onto the wealth the rich generate by diverting that wealth through taxation (income redistribution) into programs for undeserving poor people. These are people who subscribe to the quote from Abraham Lincoln, "You cannot make a weak man strong by making a strong man weak."

The countering view is that rich people exploit poor people and live lives of privilege beyond what rich people should be entitled. Those with this view point to things like how many times more the earnings of corporate Chief Executive Officers (CEOs) are in America over their workers, how the media are controlled to present the point of view of the rich and how lobbyists ensure that legislators enact pork programs and tax credits favoring the rich as examples of the view's reality.

For those of us neither exceptionally poor or rich, this raises some fundamental questions. What should someone reasonably expect as the rewards of being rich? What advantages should not be allowed? Since there are so many more without money as with money, what leverage should the poor exercise at the ballot box at the expense of the rich? I overheard someone say that the free market economy in our democracy is fueled by greed and it is the duty of government to ensure that the greed does not become excessive.

As with most things, I think the truth lies somewhere between the two extremes. Undoubtedly, there are examples of lazy and irresponsible people who lack ambition and work hardest at avoiding work. But not all people who lack wealth are lazy and shiftless. As I wrote earlier, there are many levels of ambition in life. The fact that one person has a "mom and pop" level of commerce ambition does not make that person unworthy of respect, even in comparison to an individual with an international level of ambition.

Similarly, I am certain there are greedy business owners who seek to have all they can have at the expense of everyone else around them. But this is not true of all business owners. After all, the basis of creating wealth with a business is to create and keep a customer. Creating and keeping customers requires dealing with them fairly and honestly. Saying all business owners are tyrants is just nonsense. In addition, profit is not a dirty word. We need profitable businesses to improve the quality of our lives and to grow our investment portfolios and retirement accounts. On the other hand, we have the Abramoff scandal in 2006, which clearly shows us what can happen when checks and balances are not properly applied.

An insurance company executive once told me that he saw two kinds of business owners. One kind recognized the contribution of their employees and wanted to provide the best for them in the belief that their employees gave them their competitive edge. The other kind of owner saw employees as a drain on his profits that he wanted to minimize at all costs. The second kind of employer; who refuses to share in success and pays at such an inadequate level that the employees become eligible for government support (meaning that taxpayers make up for the dollars the employer refuses to pay), is a source of the conflict.

Another source of this conflict, in my opinion, is ignorance. Ignorance of the realities of business, economics and money basics keeps many people behind on their bills and makes their dreams seem unattainable. If no one has taught you how to play the game, then you're not going to play very well. If someone does teach you how to play the game, then you can change from having poor-people problems to having rich-people problems. If you are one of those people who thinks prosperity is beyond you because unseen evil forces of the wealthy are conspiring against you and you have no responsibility for your lack of wealth, please pay attention to the next few paragraphs. If the last sentence doesn't apply to you, please skip to the next topic.

For those of you who seek wealth and don't have a personal voice of wisdom and reason to teach you these lessons, don't despair. Those voices are available in the marketplace for very reasonable investments. Find a voice with which you can harmonize and your life can change today. Let me list a few for you. (And, by the way, I don't benefit financially from telling you about any of the people I'm about to list.)

Your success in both your personal and financial life will be determined by how well you

- know and understand yourself
- get in touch with your personal motivation and
- get along with others.

The master in providing this knowledge for people is Tony Robbins. See his Web site at **www.tonyrobbins.com**.

When Jim Rohn was, as he says, "Age twenty-four, broke and behind on my big mouth promises to my wife and family, it never occurred to me to blame my personal philosophy." Now a multi-millionaire, Rohn gives back for his blessings every day. His offerings are available every day at his Web site (**www.jimrohn.com**), where you can subscribe to a free email newsletter. If you can't afford his books, then you can get them through the library. As Rohn also says, "You can't get better than free, but you have to at least be willing to go to the library and get the card."

Dave Ramsey was once seduced by the debt monster. His book, *Total Money Makeover*, is stuffed to the point of bursting with easily understandable wisdom that will enable you to defeat the debt monster and go on to achieve the financial life you want to have. Ramsey's Web site **www.daveramsey.com** will tell you how to take advantage of his wisdom, even if it's just learning by listening to his radio show.

If you prefer your wisdom in a feminine voice, then check out Suze Orman. Her Web site, like Dave Ramsey's, will offer you many different ways to tap into the knowledge she offers at **www.suzeorman.com**.

A relative newcomer is Robert T. Kiyosaki. His philosophies from his book series, *Rich Dad, Poor Dad*, have shown people a new way to think about money, cash flow and investments. His books show the reader, to paraphrase the liner notes, "What the rich teach their kids about money that the poor and middle class do not." Like the others, Kiyosaki has a Web site at **www.richdad.com**.

Of course, the book already considered a classic is Thomas J. Stanley and William D. Danko's *The Millionaire Next Door*. Their illuminating work shows that those who are millionaires often do not fit the preconceived notions the public has of them. They are more likely, as the book says, to be people who cared "not so much about keeping up with the Joneses as they did about the creation of their own personal go to hell fund." Which means they wanted a fund from which they could enable themselves to walk away from people and situations they didn't like and tell those people to go to hell.

Medical Malpractice, Medical Coverage and Litigation

Here again we have a topic that should begin with an examination grounded in economics and statistical reality. First, let's look at the economics. (Some of this may seem basic to you, but the issue has gotten to the point where we need to return to basics in order to have a reasoned discussion.) The basic law of economics is the law of supply and demand. That law says that if you take any commodity in a limited supply and increase the demand for that commodity, then the price you can charge for that commodity will go up. Let's apply that to the practice of medicine.

Becoming a medical doctor is not an easy task. Not everyone can be a doctor. The intellectual requirements are very high. We who seek medical care want our doctors to be very smart people. Nor is brainpower the only restrictive criteria to being a doctor.

What about the gifts of physical dexterity required in a surgeon? Think of the minute detail of working within the confines of the human heart. Not like hiring someone to work at a car wash, is it?

What about mental attitude and discipline? Would you want as your chosen means of making a living to have to look at (for example) different human anuses every day, day after day, with some of them diseased? I mean, why would people expose that part of their body to you unless they suspected they were diseased?

So what we have in doctors is a commodity in limited supply. The price of a commodity in limited supply will go up. And now we have a demographic in the aging of the baby boomers and the overall desire for health that increases the demand for that commodity to a level never previously reached.

Consequently, there is money to be made in the medical field. Money that is generated not just by the doctors, but by the agencies that supply the doctors with medical equipment, prescription drugs, office equipment, software, and so on. These commodities all drive the fees of medicine. Legitimate vendors are attracted when money is available, as well as scam artists.

Scams take many forms, but the ones doctors complain about the most are malpractice suits. The threat of malpractice suits causes doctors to err on the side of caution with regard to testing and procedures. This drives up the cost of medicine for all medical insurance carriers. Those insurance carriers pass these increased costs on to consumers. The increased costs cause consumers to be uninsured. The fact that so many people are uninsured results in abuse of our medical system and drives up costs again for those who still have medical insurance. A vicious cycle is created that we will discuss in a moment.

For now, let's talk about malpractice, and then go back to the vicious cycle. Despite its best efforts, the medical profession has inadequate performers in its ranks. Although I am not in favor of making it easy to sue doctors, at the same time I am not in favor of restricting the ability of the individual to gain just and fair compensation when they have been injured by medical mistakes. There is a balance point here connecting the medical community, the legal profession and the general public that is equitable for all. We need to find it.

If we can find that balance point, then perhaps medical costs can be more reasonable. And if medical costs can be more reasonable, then perhaps more people can have medical insurance, which drives down medical costs yet again. That's a good spiral.

For me, as a medical consumer, one of the drivers of medical costs seems to be the threat of catastrophic illness. Here's what I mean. Statistically, if one scans the entire population, a small number of us will enjoy total health throughout our lives and die in an accident that will kill us instantly. The health care costs of those individuals will be rock-bottom low.

By the same token, a small number of us may be involved in a catastrophic accident in which we survive, but as little more than a vegetable. In that state we consume hundreds of thousands of dollars – millions – in medical care. Consider this simple example.

Let's say 100 medical insurance companies serve the entire population of this country. Each of them has an equal share of the population. Each of them is subject to the threat of having to pay one of its customers for injuries suffered in a catastrophic accident. There might be 1,000 of these types of accidents in a year, but the insurance companies don't know which of them will be responsible for paying out for those accidents. If one insurance company had a disproportionate number of claims from those accidents, then it could be bankrupted.

Here is the point of what we're discussing. What if the government were to form an institutional insurance company to handle catastrophic medical bills? The risk of the cost of that care could be spread across the 125-million-plus households of this country at a much lower premium. For-profit medical insurance companies would be freed from charging rates to provide for the contingency of catastrophic illness, meaning more affordable rates for everyone. What's more, these more affordable rates would mean that more people could afford to have health insurance. And, if more people had health insurance, the health care providers could afford to lower their rates.

Finally, consider this idea given to me by a friend in the medical insurance industry. We require everyone who drives a car to have minimal auto insurance. Why don't we require all capable adults to have medical insurance? Instead, we have hale and hearty age 20-something folks who think they are bullet proof and refuse to divert funds to insurance. What happens when they're in a serious single car accident or get shot during a robbery and end up in the hospital? They're unable to pay. You may not think of this, but hospitals do. It's another reason hospitalization rates are so high. The more people who have at least minimal medical insurance, the lower the rates and the better off we all are. Isn't this something to strive for?

I think these ideas are worthy of examination. I hope you agree.

Environment

Biology, chemistry and the other hard sciences are not my strong suit, so this will be a basic analysis.

I am a creature of comfort. I like driving fast in air-conditioned or heated comfort. I like being able to keep my house at an agreeable temperature by adjusting a dial. I like not having to get up in the middle of the night to feed the fire before it goes out. I think indoor plumbing is one of the great inventions of mankind. I have lived in seven states and visited all but a few of the rest. I've also lived in and visited nine foreign countries. People sometimes ask me how I liked living in those places. My reply is that anywhere with flush toilets and cable TV is good with me.

What I don't like is the thought of going back to a time when horses were the means that powered our travel. The idea of mucking out the stall to get rid of the horse manure is not my idea of a good use of time. The time, labor and expense of owning and maintaining horses are simply not appealing. I've ridden in topless jeeps (the equivalent of horse-drawn wagons) in the wintertime when I was in the Army. I assure you it is not pleasant.

I like even less that we are held hostage to foreign powers and their internal political violence because we need the oil that comes from within their borders. If we are to be free of such entanglements, then we must find the alternative methods of fuel that we can produce within our own borders. And to find and produce those methods, we must weigh and perhaps overcome the voices that proclaim, "Not in my backyard!" (NIMBY).

At the same time, I feel one of our most solemn obligations as human beings is to leave this planet in as good as or better condition as when we came to it. I believe in development and economic progress balanced against the sustaining of nature.

I am very much concerned about the prospect of global warming, the melting of the polar icecap, and the seemingly resultant savagery of the 2005 hurricanes, particularly Katrina. If we are to leave this planet livable for our children and generations to come, then we must act.

Action will inevitably create costs for businesses and consumers alike, but action will also create opportunity for those providing us those services.

Somewhere between these points of view is a reasonable plan of action that will enable us to fulfill our responsibility to ourselves and our posterity.

Guns

The issue of gun ownership in our society has two distinct poles. At one pole are those who abhor the possession of firearms of any kind and argue for the most stringent restrictions possible on gun ownership. At the other pole are groups (primarily the National Rifle Association or NRA) that use the Second Amendment to the U.S. Constitution to resist any form of gun control. My personal experience in this area causes me to be of two minds.

I have friends who are missionaries in Africa. They told me once that in one of the countries where they worked, the general population was restricted from owning firearms. The paramilitary forces (a cross between the police and the military) were corrupt in that country. At night, those forces were known to force their way into private residences to rape and steal.

A short distance away was another country that had an equally corrupt paramilitary force. This country did allow the population to possess firearms. In the second country, the paramilitary forces do not force their way into private residences. Why?

Because, my friend tells me, in the second country you don't know what's on the other side of the door. In the first country, when you break down the door, all that stands between you and what you want is a club or knife. Once you get enough people in the door, it's easy to subdue whoever is wielding the club or the knife. Not so in the second country. The first guy through the door gets shot and so does everyone else until the shooter runs out of ammunition. As you might imagine, it's difficult to convince someone to be the first one through the door in the second country.

One of the most telling lines that shaped my personal philosophy is from the book and movie *Shane*. In the story, the gunfighter Shane finally succumbs to the pleading of the farmer's son to show the son how to do a fast draw. The farmer's wife catches Shane giving the lesson. "I don't want my boy to be a gunfighter," she tells Shane. Shane considers his words and then replies with something like this. "A gun is just a tool, like a shovel or an axe. It's no better, and no worse, than the man who's using it."

If you haven't as an adult watched *Shane* the movie or read the book, then I suggest you do so. You might also want to watch *Open Range*. Both these stories are about what men of principle and honor do to triumph over evil in the absence of established or the presence of corrupt law enforcement.

I do not feel firearms should be banned. I do feel, however, that gun ownership should be restricted. That restriction should be placed in such a way only those who have a record of solid citizenship free of felony criminal activity and possessing sufficient mental health to not be a threat to them or others are qualified to legally possess guns. We already say, of course, convicted felons are not worthy of our trust with regard to firearms.

I also feel part of the goal of firearms restriction should be ensuring our police are better armed than the criminals they face, not vice versa. When we continually allow civilians to upgrade the level of their weaponry in the marketplace, then we as taxpayers must foot the bill for upgrading the weaponry of those who protect us.

I appreciate that some gun enthusiasts among us are not satisfied with even the best of hunting weaponry. Yet, who among us truly needs a .50 caliber machine gun capable of shooting down airplanes? Combat weaponry should lie within the military. Perhaps a compromise might be the creation of specially licensed shooting range facilities where individuals could go to fire particularly high-powered weapons.

For those who are truly concerned for their continued freedom and safety if "only the government and criminals have guns," I recommend they read my analysis of our defense and homeland security policies later in Part Two.

Finally, for those of you who like to fish, hunt and generally enjoy undeveloped countryside, I have this thought. Beware those who would tell you to your face that they support your right to hunt, fish, and so on. Beware because those same people who tell you one thing to your face to get your vote then act to abuse that power. They abuse their power by enacting programs for the benefit of their corporate supporters. Those programs may well have a very negative impact on the habitat of the game you want to pursue. Having the best of hunting, fishing and photography equipment is useless if business activity has left no lands available for those activities. So if you are someone who enjoys the great outdoors, then you should be checking not just a candidate's NRA rating, but their environmental rating as well.

Analysis of Issues Equivalent to Prohibition

Modern issues with the magnitude of prohibition or slavery are remarkable in that they, first, revolve around the personal freedom and choices allowed to individuals and, second, often specifically involve sexual freedom.

Think about it, one of the reasons for the conflict between Western and Muslim culture is the latter's repression of sexuality and the desire by some of its elements to continue the practice. Wasn't one of the motivations for the suicide bombers the promise after death of 72 virgins in heaven?

Given that discussion, let's analyze a few of the issues that continue as a source of contention. We will not be able to move forward as a society until a clear majority view emerges that allows us to put these issues behind us.

SEVEN
NATIONAL DEFENSE AND HOMELAND SECURITY

Let's review the questions about this topic. How should we choose who fights for us? How should we determine the size and nature of our defense force? How do we determine what equipment that defense force needs? Remember that war is crime on a larger scale. We would not abolish our police departments. We cannot abolish our military. How do we integrate homeland security into the national defense equation? How do we decide which conflicts are worth fighting and which are not? How do we balance our desire for security with maintenance of our rights as citizens of this country?

As I write this in 2006, America is past the third anniversary of its involvement in Iraq. Even at this stage, people are looking back and asking, "Where did we go wrong and what do we need to do to keep this situation from arising again?"

Answering these questions requires a perspective on American history, particularly from World War I forward. I will attempt to provide that perspective with a brief overview.

As another native Missourian, President Harry S. Truman, was fond of saying, "There's really nothing new in the world. There's only all the history you don't know."

The history you may not know

World War I began in August 1914 when a series of treaty obligations was initiated by a single political assassination that snowballed into a full-scale mobilization of Europe. America struggled to remain free of that war, but was finally drawn in during 1917. That year saw the raising of the American forces through a conscription program using a lottery mechanism. By 1918, America is fully involved in the fighting, which ended at the 11th hour of November 11, 1918. The peace accords, which are signed the following June, failed to incorporate the magnanimous terms of President Woodrow Wilson's 14 Points. Among those 14 Points was a vision for the creation of a League of Nations as a body to prevent similar wars in the future.

The way World War I ended sowed the seeds for the rise of fascism in Germany and Italy. The failure of the winning powers of World War I to assert themselves enabled Adolph Hitler to rearm his country and launch Germany's invasion of Poland in August 1939. Germany quickly overran the rest of Western Europe and subjected Britain to a vicious air campaign in an attempt to gain her surrender. (The air campaign failed.)

Two-plus years later America was finally brought into this war with the Japanese attack on Pearl Harbor in December

1941. Once again, treaty alliances between countries (Germany's pact with Japan required Germany to declare war on America after Pearl Harbor) caused America to declare war on the Axis powers. The size of the effort needed to win meant (despite the number of volunteers that enlisted) conscription was instituted again to raise the numbers needed for victory. The massive war effort was supported by all levels of society because of the commonly accepted vision that the American way of life was profoundly threatened by the Axis powers. All levels of society in America sacrificed not just material wealth and comfort, but the members of their families. Among those serving were the grandson of Teddy Roosevelt and six men who would eventually become President of the United States (Dwight D. Eisenhower, John F. Kennedy, Richard M. Nixon, Gerald Ford, Ronald Reagan and George H. W. Bush).

The carnage from this war was staggering. The cost in both human life and material was absolutely enormous. Just to give a comparison in scale (and realizing that no death is insignificant), America lost 7,000 dead in just 38 days of combat to take the island of Iwo Jima in WWII. As I write this, America has lost over 2,500 dead in 40 months of combat in Iraq. Are the intensities of those two wars different? Absolutely, but (to reiterate) I'm quoting those numbers to you to give you a sense of scale. How intense was combat in WWII? While I wasn't there personally, I think we can all agree that the opening of the movie *Saving Private Ryan* gives all of us a strong sense of that intensity.

Lessons learned from WWII

In the aftermath of WWII, certain lessons learned came to have almost universal acceptance. Foremost among those lessons is that appeasement of tyranny does not work. America could no longer afford to stand back and let things get out of control as they had in the two world wars. When America gets involved (so went the thinking) things get resolved. Look at the timelines leading to that thinking. WWI started late 1914, America got involved late in 1917, and the war is over by November 1918. WWII starts August 1939, America gets involved by almost 1942, and the war is over in August 1945. So we as a nation decide to be involved on the world stage in several ways.

First, in hindsight, we decide President Wilson was right about the League of Nations idea, and we support the creation of the United Nations. Second, we institute the Marshall Plan to rebuild Europe in a way we hoped would forestall future conflicts. Third, we declare our willingness to get involved early in a conflict while that conflict is small in order to keep the conflict small.

Our initial test of that doctrine was the invasion of South Korea by North Korea. Despite an early lack of military preparedness, we were able to restore the boundary between the two countries. (Continuous military preparedness was another lesson of WWII, but one this country has difficulty executing in times of diminished threats.) In doing so, we hopefully have learned (among other lessons) that we may need to think more deeply about the implications of what is called "Limited War."

Limited War, in contrast to our two previous wars, is fought with a goal short of getting the outright surrender of our opponent. America also learns that fighting a Limited War may also expand beyond its intended scope by reason of causing another opponent to enter the battle. Such was the case in Korea when the Red Chinese decided to join the North Koreans because of the threat to their own borders the Chinese perceived as America drove through North Korea.

The Chinese were formidable opponents. Veterans of that war have told of the human wave charges the Chinese would mount. Only the front ranks would have rifles and the rest would have clubs. When our soldiers shot the Chinese with rifles, the ones with clubs would pick up the rifles and keep coming. Our forces would fire machine guns with such intensity that the barrels would droop like candles from the heat of firing. And yet the Chinese would keep coming. From this experience came the desire to keep the Chinese uninvolved in any other war we should fight in the future. This would be one of the factors that would severely limit our operations in Vietnam. The raising of manpower for the Korean War was done through enlistment, the Draft, and the activation and deployment of Reserve and National Guard forces. Owing to the proximity to WWII, little resentment was expressed in opposition against this approach.

Where have all the recruits gone?

In the years between the end of active hostilities in Korea and the ramp-up of forces in Vietnam, fewer males were needed for military service requirements. While all males between the ages of 18 and 26 had a military service obligation and were required to have a draft card, not all males would actually serve. Exemptions to military service were routinely granted for being enrolled in college, for married men with children or not passing a physical or mental examination. Being homosexual would also keep you from serving in the military, but (societal disfavor being what it was) few males at the time would admit that was the case to avoid service. In general, if you could afford to go to college, then you were highly unlikely to be called for military service.

Reams and reams of material have been written about the political, strategic and tactical errors made in the conduct of the Vietnam War. Suffice to say America tried to apply the lessons of WWII in Europe to an Asian situation and miscalculated what was needed to prevail. In the process, the trust between the government and the people who elected its representatives was severely damaged. The factors that caused that damage had a great deal to do with how the forces were raised for Vietnam.

The first of these factors was the President's having the authority to expand and deploy active duty troop organizations without involving Reserve and National Guard units. This created a safe haven for the children of the well-to-do and well-connected to fulfill their military obligation with a significantly lessened threat to life and limb involved. This also meant American life went on pretty much as usual because people were not being wrenched away from their primary means of making a living to fight a war. As a result, there was little debate in the early years of Vietnam as to whether this escalation was the best way to get the result America most desired in Southeast Asia.

The second of these factors was that the manpower requirement grew so big the children of the middle class began to be drafted. At the peak of the Vietnam expansion, a common experience was to have finished four years of college and be drafted. The middle class was populated with a great number of veterans as parents. At first, these parents were highly supportive of the war because of their belief the war was necessary in order to avoid appeasement and confront communism. As the war dragged on without a clear objective and exit strategy, support began to wane.

The third of these factors was the students with deferments and their reaction to the war. That reaction was fed by their peers who first did a tour in Vietnam, were discharged and then came to the campus. The students who had not been to Vietnam did not like the descriptions of the war being told to them by those who had already been there. The students' active and vocal protests called attention to the inadequacies of how the war was being fought and further soured the American public on continuing that war.

Revamping the Draft via lottery

The unfairness of the Draft's conduct led to its revamping in the late 1960s. A lottery format was instituted. Two giant cages that could be spun around and the contents mixed were used. One cage had small individual capsules with all the individual dates for the coming year (March 22, June 2, and so on). The other cage's capsules were the numbers 1 through 365 (366 for a leap year). People would come out on the stage and pick one date and then one sequence number. If the date picked was your birthday and the sequence number for your birthday was number 1, then you were in a group that was the first choice of the government to be considered for military service.

No one would be called for military service with a sequence number higher than "1" until all the "1s" had been called. Conversely, if your sequence number was 365, then national circumstances would have to be bad for you to be called. This was a highly impartial system for all concerned. If the Draft were to be re-instituted in this country, then this is the system that would be used. But the well-to-do and the well-connected didn't like this system. This system offered no exemptions from military service (especially when coupled with another later change I will describe in a moment). So it was in the early 1970s that America transformed its military recruitment to an all-volunteer basis.

In the aftermath of Vietnam, then Chief of Staff of the Army (General Creighton Abrams) and key members of Congress set out to arrange the military differently. Their goal was to set up the structure of the military so that no President could commit America to a long-term, large-scale military involvement without the involvement of the Reserve and the National Guard. To accomplish this, the combat fighting units were predominantly placed in the active forces and the service and support units (trucks, supply, graves registration) in the Reserve and National Guard. The intent of this structure was to ensure that if a long-term, large-scale military operation were proposed, then an intensive debate would be sparked about the worthiness of that operation by interrupting business as usual in American life. This also meant the Reserve and the National Guard units were no longer a safe haven to avoid combat. This removal is the later change I referred to in the previous paragraph.

The current Bush Administration, as I will describe later, has managed to circumvent those safeguards.

In the aftermath of Vietnam, military problems with people, organization and equipment continued. For example, in the early 1980s the number of North Atlantic Treaty Organization (NATO) tanks compared to the number of Soviet (Warsaw Pact) tanks gave the Soviets a 5-1 advantage.

The 1980 Desert One fiasco attempting the rescue of the American Embassy hostages from Iran illuminated problems in Force and Command Structure. The problems illuminated by that failure led to the passage of the Goldwater-Nichols Bill. That bill gave the U.S. the organization that resulted in the Gulf War One victory.

The continuing people problem

People continued to be a problem. Pay in the late 1970s and early 1980s, the primary incentive for recruiting people in an all-volunteer military, was abysmal. One of the unwritten administrative skills for Non Commissioned Officers (NCOs) was to be able to instruct subordinate married enlisted personnel how to apply for food stamps. In order to fill the ranks, recruiters were authorized to sign people who fell into what was known as Mental Category Four. Category Four personnel are not bright people; they require extra training, extra supervision and are prone to disciplinary problems.

The coming of the Reagan Administration began to address some of these issues. Pay rates were boosted and a new GI Bill program was instituted at the same time that availability of student loan money was restricted. In effect, the Reagan Administration said to young people, "We won't loan you money for college directly, but you can earn it through military service." The result was that by the mid-80s many of the lower-ranking enlisted personnel (particularly in the Army) were smarter than the NCOs from whom the enlistees took orders. In essence, America went from a political draft to an economic draft in order to entice the personnel needed to fill the ranks of its military.

The downside to this system was the uncertainty as to what would happen if America became involved in a large-scale, long-term conflict that was not quite big enough to spark reactivation of the Draft. Would the financial incentives be enough to keep the recruiting pipeline full in the face of significant casualties and still maintain the quality of troops? The answer given: America would deal with the problem if it came.

The Reagan Administration took other positive steps as well. They made the investments needed in equipment for all the services to counter the Soviet Union. This was one of several factors eventually leading to the collapse of the Soviet Union because it could not afford to monetarily keep up with the military spending of America.

After an initial misstep in Lebanon in 1983, the Administration's Secretary of Defense, Casper Weinberger, developed the Weinberger Doctrine. This doctrine was further refined by the Powell Doctrine (so named for its author, General Colin Powell). The essence of these two doctrines sets a standard for determining whether or not the United States should commit to using military force. A key tenet of the two doctrines is that if America goes to war, then America should go to war to win.

The worthiness of those two doctrines was proven in two conflicts during the Bush I Administration. Those two conflicts were our incursion into Panama in 1989 and Gulf War I in 1990-1991. Both these conflicts were over and done with quickly with minimum casualties to U.S. troops.

The approaching day of reckoning

As I write this, the day of reckoning has come on how we fill the ranks of our Armed Forces, particularly the Army. Enlistment goals were not being met and only rebounded when standards were lowered to once again accept category 4 enlistees. As a result, actions are being taken that are not in the long-term interest of America or the Army as an institution. In order to stop the loss of soldiers needed at a critical time, the Army is invoking a clause in enlistment contracts called (aptly enough) Stop Loss. America had a similar policy in effect in WWII, but such a policy was appropriate for WWII. Americans understood that each was committed to the war effort until they died or the Axis powers were defeated. Americans in WWII had a sense of shared sacrifice and commitment. That situation does not exist today.

We are a nation of over 286 million people as of the 2000 Census (recent estimates are that the figure has now passed 300 million). According to one official Army source, there are more than 600,000 soldiers on active duty in 2006. The Marines have authorized end strength of 178,000. (Not to denigrate the other services, but the war on terror is primarily a land-based war fought by soldiers and Marines, and the other services are not being impacted by Stop Loss.) That means that less than 1 percent (.27 percent, to be precise) is defending the other 99 percent of Americans not on active duty. Let's ask ourselves this question. What kind of a nation have we become when we force the few unlucky enough to be on active duty to face death over and over while others capable of service are allowed to escape facing this kind of risk?

As I have stated, another action being taken is the reduction of standards for enlistment. We are now once again allowing Category Four personnel in the force. One wonders about the possible connection between this decision and recent news reports of crimes committed by service members in Iraq, as well as the notation that Aryan Nation graffiti is now seen in Iraq.

Still other actions are being taken that disguise the true manpower needs and costs of the so-called war on terror. I saw a *Frontline* program on PBS about the use of "contractors" in Iraq, particularly the so-called security companies. Let's call those folks what they are – mercenaries. Based on data from the *Frontline* program, I estimated we're paying 10 of the mercenaries for a year in Iraq about $2.16 million. We pay a 10-man rifle squad (pay and allowances plus combat pay) about $293,000 for the same time in country. The mercenaries get seven times more money.

I brought this up with some contacts I made in the Government Accounting Office (GAO). They pointed out that I wasn't accounting for all the cost factors, and the true cost of 10 soldiers for a year in Iraq was closer to $1 million before combat pay was calculated.

I appreciate cost accounting and the fact the cost of people in uniform goes beyond their direct pay and allowances. At the same time, I noted their comparison did not factor in the additional costs of contracting the security firm. I was only noting the costs of direct pay to the individuals. What's more, I was calculating the pay to the contractors using the lowest rate of $600 a day quoted in the Frontline program.

If I calculate based on the mid-range rate, the pay to 10 contractors for a year would be $2,920,000, not including the other cost factors of contracting with the security company in the first place. If I use the GAO's full cost accounting figure of $1 million for 10 soldiers plus their combat pay of around $300,000, we have an imperfect comparison $2.9 million to $1.3 million. We are still willing to pay mercenaries twice what we are willing to pay soldiers.

But what we pay, in my opinion, is not the true issue. I am pointing out another set of issues that should concern all Americans.

Shared sacrifice

We are fighting an insurgency in Iraq. One key to defeating an insurgency is to put a 10 to 1 force ratio in the field. Why are we willing to pay mercenaries to fight for us, but not willing to pay soldiers in sufficient numbers to do the job?

Has our reliance on an all-volunteer military twisted our paradigm so badly we have lost the concept of the citizen-soldier? Have we lost the sense of shared sacrifice? I fear the answer to those questions is yes. As I wrote before, we do not have an all-volunteer military. We have a recruited military. The difference should be obvious.

I feel the Bush Administration is using contractors to avoid tripping the circuit breakers incorporated in the integration of the Reserves and National Guard into the Total Force Structure. The circuit breaker mechanism developed by General Creighton Abrams and key members of Congress as a reaction to Vietnam has been bypassed by the use of contractors, and we find ourselves in a very Vietnam-like way in Iraq. (See my separate dialogue, The Unspeakable Iraq Option, at the end of this chapter. There I discuss the fact that America is short some 70,000 soldiers to make a military solution work.)

Why, after all this history and all these lessons learned do we find ourselves bogged down in Iraq? And, make no mistake, we are bogged down. The reason is we have never insisted on implementing a system that takes advantage of two of the great truisms in life. Here are those truisms.

- Money talks and Bulls**t walks.
- For where your treasure is, there your heart will be also. (Matthew 6:21)

Here is what I think these truisms mean to us and how they relate to the history I have thus far provided you.

First, let's analyze what I mean by "Money talks and Bulls**t walks." If you are an average American like me, what do you think will happen if you call your Congressperson on the phone and ask to speak with him or her, regardless of whether the Congressperson is available or not? You're going to be told that the Congressperson is not available, but thank you very much for your call. The person at the congressional office will duly note your message/concern. Eventually, you will get a written response. Not being able to speak personally with your Congressional representation may not happen 100 percent of the time, but 85 to 90 percent sounds reasonable.

Let's change the scenario a bit. You are a major contributor to your Congressperson's campaigns. You call and ask to speak with the Congressperson and the Congressperson is available. What do you think your chances are of speaking with the Congressperson now? I'd say the percentages reverse. You have an 85 percent chance of speaking with your representative and only a 15 percent chance of being told that the Congressperson is unavailable. And, even if you don't get through, you won't get a letter in return. You'll get a call.

I'm not saying there is anything necessarily wrong with

what I've just described. This is the way of the world. You and I are not going to change it. Instead of trying to change it, however, we need to set up a system to harness it.

Where your treasure is

Let's go to my other truism; "For where your treasure is, there your heart will be also." Here is what I think this means to us.

Most people think of treasure in terms of items of wealth. But people who are healthy mentally don't love things or money. They love what money can do for them and the people they love. Why are ransoms paid for people who are kidnapped? Because people love the person who is kidnapped more than they love the money it takes to pay the ransom.

Would you voluntarily pay for a life insurance policy for someone who was not a member of your family? The answer is basically no, isn't it? Oh, you might in a business sense pay for key person insurance in a business setting. If you did pay for key person insurance, then you did so because you recognized the loss of that person would threaten the continued profitability of the business. And you reasoned loss of profitability would affect the health and welfare of your loved ones.

Why bring this up?

Because we have had the lapses in military readiness in equipment and personnel in this country because the general population was unwilling to pay the premium on the insurance policy a ready military represents. I further think the reason there was unwillingness to pay the premium is that families of influence too often had none of their own family at personal risk through military service.

Let's be direct.

If the lottery Draft had been put in place in the aftermath of September 11, 2001, and—

If that Draft were administered in such a way that the sons and daughters, nieces and nephews, and grandchildren of all the Members of Congress, the Supreme Court, the Executive Branch, and the top officers and members of the Boards of Directors of the Fortune 500 were at equal risk to see their children at war losing their limbs and lives to IEDs (Improvised Explosive Devices) in Iraq as the children of the disadvantaged and poor in this country—

Would this country be in Iraq today?*

I submit the answer is no.

When the war drums were being beaten in the fall of 2002 and the winter of 2003, no calls were being made by people with the power to get their calls returned. Those who had that power did not have their treasure at risk. Those with money did not talk and bullsh**t, therefore, walked us into Iraq.

---

* Please note: I am not saying there are zero members of the groups named above in uniform fighting for our freedom. They are represented and have suffered loss. My respect and my condolences go out to them in the sincerest way. That's not my point. My point is this. Those groups collectively do not feel or fear the threat of the loss of their treasure. This lack of fear must be replaced with an equitable means of generating shared sacrifice at all levels of society.

Not your father's war

I have noted President Bush and his immediate subordinates in the Department of Defense (DOD) have compared the war on terror to the magnitude of our conflict in WWII. With the recent attacks by Israel on Lebanon, we now have a new term – World War III. If that comparison is valid, then I have a question for the President: Why aren't your daughters in uniform?

Think about it. If we are truly in a state of emergency equal to World War II, then why isn't the entire nation being called on for sacrifice? Why isn't the Draft operating again to replace the casualties we're taking? Why are we tolerating shortages of personnel in the Army? Why aren't the wealthiest Americans being asked to pay more taxes instead of being given more and more tax breaks? Why is the country being allowed to sink deeper and deeper into debt to foreign countries?

If we are not truly in a state of WWII-like emergency, then I can think of only two answers to these questions. Either those whom we have elected to lead us are grossly incompetent, or there is no true national emergency and an act of savagery by a band of zealots in September 2001 is being leveraged to provide a smokescreen behind which appalling injustices are being allowed to take place.

At this point, you may be wondering, "When (or how) is this topic going to be analyzed with the methodology the other topics were subjected to?" Good question. Let's do so.

National security and homeland defense has become the ultimate monkey-head issue. The American population has had the fear card played on it like one of Pavlov's experiments to enable the narrow agenda of a warped few to be implemented.

What the current prophets bring us

The Bible tells us that Jesus warned his disciples of false prophets and told them how to identify them. "Beware of false prophets, who come to you in sheep's clothing, but inwardly are ravening wolves. By their fruits you will know them." (Matthew 15 & 16) By fruits, the Bible means results. Let's look at the results the current prophets are bringing us with their policies.

- Record high gas prices
- A crisis in immigration and border control
- On the path to losing a costly war with no reasonable end in sight
- A bungled response to one of the worst hurricanes on record
- The highest debt our nation has ever endured I could go on, but isn't this enough?

Does this war affect you physically, mentally/emotionally, or financially? There are several ways to answer this question.

This war affects you physically if you have to fight in it. And if you have to fight in it, then the war certainly affects you mentally/emotionally for obvious reasons. Financially, the war affects you most if you are a Reservist or National

Guardsman called to active duty and forced to give up a paycheck that supported your family for one that does not. Financially, the war affects each and every one of us because the Bush Administration is fighting this war not by raising and then spending sufficient current revenues, but by running up the figurative credit card and not collecting adequate taxes. Someday, for us, our children and their children, there will be a reckoning for this irresponsibility.

This war does not affect you physically if you don't have to fight in it unless you know someone who has to fight in it and especially if that person is someone you love. In that case, worry has some physical effects, and grief, if warranted, definitely has physical effects. Clearly, in those circumstances, there are mental/emotional impacts. The potential for financial impacts exist, as well. What if the loved one fails to return and the loved one left behind has to raise a child without the additional income of a two-parent household?

But what is your attitude and your perspective if you yourself are not fighting, have never fought in anything similar yourself and you know of no one who is fighting?   The fight doesn't affect you physically, does it?   Nor does it affect you mentally/emotionally, because no one that you love is at risk. Even if you are a person of wealth, the war does not affect you financially (except in the global sense I described earlier). The war is just one more threat to your wealth with which you deal every day. Your true treasure is not at risk and will not be at risk unless you have a loved one who decides that enlisting is a good idea.

Let's be blunt. Without a draft, my best estimate is that the majority of America's population fits into this third category. This is what we need to change.

Why do we find ourselves as we are in Iraq?

Because our current system of raising and maintaining our military made creating that situation possible, particularly for people who came to power with an agenda. We lacked the motivation required to implement fully the checks and balances necessary to investigate truly whether the course of action proposed was the right one. And (in my opinion) we will continue to lack those checks and balances until we return to a system of staffing our military that subjects **all** members of that society to the risks of fighting its wars.

Much has been made of botched or manipulated intelligence and its contribution to the decision to go to war in Iraq. Our system of a recruited military had an impact there, as well. Consider this explanation.

For intelligence to be of value against potential adversaries, what your side knows about its adversaries must necessarily be limited to those with a need to know that information. In a democracy, the electorate must trust that the elected will use intelligence in a proper way. If the electorate demands that the intelligence be revealed to the general public, then intelligence has no value at all. For the electorate to trust that intelligence is being used properly, the electorate has the right to expect that their elected representatives will suffer equally with them if the actions taken in response to the intelligence is wrong. If that expectation is not there, then the electorate cannot trust its elected representatives.

Further, if the elected representatives demonstrate that they failed to apply intelligence properly, then those representatives should be held accountable by being turned out of office. (As an aside, note the following: I asked a member of Congress what level of security clearance he had. I was told that he had been given a Top Secret clearance just by virtue of being elected. A Congressperson, therefore, should have as much access to intelligence as any member of the Executive Branch.)

In one sense, as voters, our situation with regard to Iraq is similar to that of a member of the board of directors of a bank. Think of what you would do if you discovered yourself in the following situation.

You find out one of your loan officers has had a personal relationship with a local businessman. That relationship has been leveraged in such a way that the loan officer has made a questionable loan. The businessman, either through deceit or incompetence, has failed to judge the true costs of the project he got the loan for. Now the businessman is back asking for more money. If the additional loan is not granted, then the entire project will fail. In fact, even if you grant the loan, the loan does not guarantee that the project will be successful. If the project fails even with the additional funds, then you are throwing good money after bad. Your loss will be even bigger than it potentially is now. Once the loss comes to light, not only will your competitors use it against you in gaining customers, but you will have to charge higher rates to make up for the loss. That would make you less competitive in the marketplace. To complicate matters, the businessman hints that if you don't loan him the money, he will go elsewhere to get the money and thereby let it be known that yours is a less than efficient bank. What do you do?

Were I a director at this bank, I would take three actions.

- First, I would dismiss the current loan officer.

- Second, I would institute oversight procedures to prevent a repetition of the situation.

- Third, I would probably let the businessman have the additional funding if the businessman would agree to my terms. Those terms would be a higher interest rate, incremental issuance of the funds instead of all at once and agreement to oversight of the project. I would insist on the hiring of a consultant agreeable to me (whose fees are paid by the businessman) to oversee the day-to-day operations. If the consultant sees something the bank would not like, then we immediately come to a meeting. If the situation can't be resolved, then I would cut off further funding.

In this way, I would hope to protect the bank's interests and do my utmost to insure the success of the project so the bank can get its money back. My feeling would be that the businessman's threats to expose the original loans are empty. The businessman does not want it widely known that he is either (a) incompetent or (b) a crook. One thing more is certain. Once I had my money back from this businessman, I would never do business with him again.

Examine the true costs

Here is how this relates to our situation in Iraq. We have someone in charge of a project who, through deceit or incompetence, has failed to judge the true costs of the project. That person expects us to continue to pay for their project, no matter what the cost. Approval for this project was facilitated by a crony relationship – that is, a Republican-controlled Congress and a system without proper checks and balances.

As a voter, I am as obligated as the member of the board of directors to take action to preserve the integrity of my institution. In this case, the institution is the Republic of the United States of America. As a voter, I want to take the following actions to preserve that Republic.

First, I would replace the current members of Congress with those who are willing to do two things. One, provide active critical oversight of the Executive Branch. Second, institute a lottery system for staffing our military. In *United We Serve*, no less than the Honorable John Lehman, former Secretary of the Navy under Ronald Reagan, noted, "Edward Gibbon wrote in *The Decline and Fall of the Roman Empire* that Rome fell when the most talented and well educated young Romans no longer served their time in the Roman cavalry."

Even if a draft (as Lehman further writes) only takes one out of 30 18-year-olds, I think that is worthwhile. I think it's worthwhile because all 30 of the parents must behave as though their child will be the one in 30 chosen. And somewhere among that set of parents will be someone who has the ability to call their Congressperson and get a return call. Someone who will tell the Congressperson (and even a President or Vice President) using language worthy of a Federal Communications Commission profanity fine they had better be sure of their facts before they start the military adventure being considered. A number of people like this can be part of a chorus that will counter flawed group-think on critical issues.

A lottery system can help us return to the concept of the citizen-soldier. We can avoid the feelings of guilt from knowing that those who fight for us are doing so largely for economic reasons. The lottery is an instrument of fairness unsurpassed by all other mechanisms.

Another side benefit America will see is one the Greatest Generation of WWII had. Military service enabled people from Minnesota, for example, to know someone from Alabama. People who would otherwise have never traveled more than 100 miles from where they were born were actually forced to live hundreds of miles away in other time zones. The broadening of their personalities from this experience, added to the appreciation they had for the fact they were still alive when the shooting stopped, enabled that generation to create what we have today. Are we going to do something to honor their memory and their sacrifice or are we just going to wimp out?

The sacred cows

I predict one other thing will happen if America adopts lottery-based conscription. The sacred cows will come up onto the negotiating table. We will get serious about energy independence in America. As others such as the *New York Times* columnist Tom Friedman have said, achieving energy independence will do some very desirable things for this country. First, it will enable this country to tell the Middle Eastern and other oil-exporting countries to go to hell, because we don't need them anymore. Those countries will still need us and our assets, but we won't need them. Second, the declining revenues from oil will starve the jihads' movements. Third, the lowered thirst for oil will help to defuse a potential conflict with nations such as China and India.

To be sure, if we go back to a lottery conscription system, then some changes will have to be made to make the system work. Let's talk about a few of those changes.

We will need to get back to an attitude we had in this country in the time of WWII and Korea. The attitude toward those who served was different. Soldiers were not expected to be paid much, especially at the lower ranks. They were going through a period of service to the country after which they were free to pursue wealth in a free market economy. If something happened to soldiers physically during that service, the country promised them a lifetime of financial support and medical care as manifested by the Veterans Administration structure we have even today.

Certainly not all soldiers will be drafted. We will still have those who volunteer with the intention of making the military a career and those who do volunteer should be paid at a higher rate. But we need to re-discover an attitude toward and by our young people that says you cannot expect to live here in America your entire life with no costs paid to maintain freedom.

We need to get away from this drift toward mercenaries with their loyalties to the highest bidders and replace it with a reaffirmation of the citizen-soldier whose loyalty is to the Republic and the Constitution. Otherwise, those of you especially who espouse the value of the Second Amendment could well see the value of that Amendment put to the test somewhere in the future. Put more plainly, those who bear arms in America's defense must come from our midst in a way that they are sure of the illegality of an order to use those arms to subjugate the citizens of America and will resist such an order en masse.

Homosexuality can no longer be a barrier to service. Somewhere I read that Barry Goldwater said something like, "I fail to see what sexual orientation has to do with the ability to sight a weapon on another human being and kill them." Besides that, do you want someone to avoid service strictly on a claim of homosexuality? What kind of test can you administer to confirm or deny homosexuality?

The system we use must provide that no one who fails any kind of mental aptitude test for military service should be subsequently allowed to enroll in a four-year college or university. The failed test can be retaken and the ban on enrollment lifted only after successful completion of the service requirement.

What if the individual who is, for example, the number one rated high school running back prospect at Rivals.com also has the number one draft number? Such individuals should have a choice of forestalling college for a two-year enlistment or going through their institution's ROTC program with a three-year active duty obligation immediately after leaving college with a commission (which means delaying entry into the NFL for three years). If they leave college without a degree or a commission, then they go directly to the military for their two-year enlistment. The nation comes first, their sport comes second. Oh, and by the way, no semi-pro teams are to be sponsored or funded by the military.

Somewhere there is a mother reading this and she is screaming, "Not my Johnny! Not my Susie!" If you're that mother, then consider this. If you want your child to grow up in freedom, then someone's child must fight. And somewhere another mother shares your anxiety (that mother might even be you). That mother is one who either has the ability to call their Congressperson's office and get the call returned or that mother has a relationship with someone else who can call their Congressperson's office and get the call returned. This is the dynamic that is needed to keep us out of unnecessary wars.

I also emphasize that we need to use the lottery system to go beyond pure military combat service. What if those who are unqualified to fight were placed as teacher's assistants to aid in education or other anti-poverty projects?

Or maybe we need to install a totally volunteer system using the system envisioned in Robert Heinlein's *Starship Troopers*. In that fictional story of the future, all service was absolutely voluntary. Service was possible no matter your physical or mental infirmity, and service went far beyond military positions. The catch was, however, that if you did not serve, then you could not vote or hold office. If such a system were implemented today without a grandfather clause, three quarters of our Congress and our current Vice President would be forced to return to the civilian careers from which they came.

Much of what I have written is, I'm sure, shocking to many of you. But what I recommend is needed. We must get rid of do-as-I-say-and-not-as-I-do leadership. We must make sure that the privilege of wealth does not include the avoidance of sacrifice for the Republic and its freedom.

Someday, there will be a meeting in the hereafter between those of you reading these words and those who came before us and gave us the freedom we have at this moment. When that meeting takes place, I want it to come with a nod and a thumbs-up that we did the right thing. I don't want it to be with a curse and shaking of heads that we didn't have the guts to keep the freedom they gave us by doing what is right and what is fair.

The Unspeakable Iraq Option

So far, I have presented "lessons learned" for future conflicts. Let us now address the question of the unspeakable Iraq option. What do we do about the situation we're in now? Unnoticed is a 600-pound gorilla of an option that no one admits seeing.

Let me present a perspective on this war not vetted by either the news media or the nation's major political parties. I call it the Gorilla option. This provides you a clear view of the actual costs of pursuing a purely military solution you are not getting from the news or our leadership. The choices we face are much more complex than "stay the course" or "withdraw ASAP."

To accomplish this, let me describe two common things in everyday life most of us understand and then relate the two to a war that most of us say we understand, but don't. The bottom line: We are losing because our political leadership is not fighting decisively to win. Our troops, on the other hand, are fighting to win, but not being given the tools with which to win.

Here is my first "common thing." Imagine yourself flying in a helicopter watching a large freight train trying to make it up and over a big hill. The engine pulling the train lacks the horsepower on its own to make it over that hill. Instead, the wheels spin and the train is not moving. The options seem pretty clear: Send for another engine from the town you just left or ask the town ahead to send out another engine and give you the additional horsepower you need. Those are the best options.

The problem is, as you look out toward the horizon from your helicopter, you see a tidal wave bearing down on the train. The train's engineer only has two options. If the additional engines cannot reach the train and pull it to safety before the tidal wave hits, then the engine must leave the cargo behind and climb the hill to safety to be able to continue to pull cargo later on.

Here is how my freight train example relates to Iraq. The engine is the military combat power we have in Iraq. That engine is not strong enough to pull its cargo (the people of Iraq) out of the town of Tyranny, over the plains of Chaos, and up and over the mountain of Transition to the destination of Stable Republic. Ask yourself these questions. If over the last three years we had had and had now sufficient combat power in Iraq to win and withdraw—

- Would insurgent activity be increasing or decreasing?

- Would Iraqi oil production be at or above prewar levels, or below?

- Would electrical power production be at or above prewar levels, or below?

- Would unemployment in Iraq be rising or falling?

Obviously, if we were winning and making progress toward withdrawing, it follows, then, that insurgent activity would be decreasing, the oil and electricity production would be at or above, and unemployment would be declining. The reality of the answers to each of those questions lets us know we are not achieving the goal we want to achieve.

Immediately, three questions probably come to mind. The first: Is this just another guy who focuses on the doom and gloom and not the good news from Iraq? The second: why, after three years of expending blood and treasure, are we in this situation? Third: what do we need to turn things around? Let's address the first question by describing my other "common thing" to help understand the situation.

Fighting a war is like building a bridge to cross over a river of conflict from a state of war to a state of peace. A real bridge enables you to cross a physical barrier. A metaphorical bridge enables you to cross over the hostility of your enemy by defeating that enemy.

Imagine the work of a bridge building company whose task is to build a bridge across a river. The point of construction is where the banks of the river are too far apart for the deck of the bridge (the span) to rest on just the river banks themselves. Instead, they must build a support structure in the middle of the river on which the main span must rest on. That support structure is called a pier. You see these piers in the form of big concrete posts in the median every day when you drive under a freeway overpass. How easy it must be to build that pier on dry land, how hard it is to build it in the middle of a river.

As you observe the company at work, you note key items. The work on the opposite banks is going well, but the crews there have the advantage of basing their work from dry land. The erection of the pier is absolutely critical to success. Without the pier, there will be no bridge. Without the bridge, there will be no traffic across the bridge, the ultimate goal of building the bridge in the first place. Without the pier, the two emplacements on the opposite banks becomes a monument to lack of proper planning, commitment and adequate resources. Those responsible for the construction of a monument instead of a bridge will be eternally associated with the words incompetence and defeat.

In Iraq, the equivalent of the pier is the defeat of

the "insurgents." That will be the hard thing to do. When you hear people whimper and whine about why the news agencies don't report the "good" news, then here is a suggested reply. "I don't care about good news because right now the only good news is the news about how we're doing on the equivalent of the embankments. I expect us to do well at building the embankments. The hard part is building the pier. Right now the news is not good about building the pier. Remember, no pier, no bridge. That's the crux for the whole project. We win or lose based on how we do building the pier – in other words, defeating the insurgency."

So now let's go to the second question. Why are we, after three years of expending blood and treasure, in this situation? The simple reason, we do not have and have not had enough soldiers on the ground to win.

When T. R. Fehrenbach published his classic critique of the Korean War *(This Kind of War)* in 1963, he wrote the following, "You may fly over a land forever; you may bomb it, atomize it, pulverize it, and wipe it clean of life – but if you desire to defend it, protect it, and keep it for civilization, you must do this on the ground, the way the Roman Legions did, by putting your young men into the mud."

We are fighting an insurgency. Current unclassified estimates put the number of insurgents at 15,000 to 20,000. The rule of thumb I learned as an Army officer for number of troops needed to counter an insurgency is 10 soldiers for every insurgent. That means we need 200,000 troops in Iraq. We have about 130,000. This is the equivalent of playing 11-man football with only seven players on your team. How many games do you think you will win playing 11 on 7, regardless of the skill and dedication of your players?

Here is the Gorilla option. If the level of effort you have in place now isn't enough to win and you want to win, you must increase your level of effort. That sounds simple, but where are the additional 70,000 soldiers going to come from – the soldiers you need to make this option work?

The Bush Administration thinks the soldiers will come from the Iraqis themselves. But will they come in sufficient numbers in time to defeat an insurgency tidal wave that grows larger and bolder every day and threatens to become a full-scale civil war? That is gambling with success. If I must gamble, then I want the odds loaded in my favor to the nth degree. The current approach does not offer this comfort level, and we can't take the "train" back to 2003 and start over.

Can we get the troops from our Allies (bring an engine from the town ahead)? That bridge has already been burned by the arrogance of the Bush Administration, and our Allies are perfectly happy to let us stew in our own juice, thank you very much.

Can we get the troops from our Reserves and National Guard forces (bring an engine from the town behind)? We have already been to that well and the water level is now very, very low. (There's a sidebar earlier in this chapter about why we are using our Reserves in the way we are as a result of our lessons learned in Vietnam and how the Bush Administration has managed to circumvent the safety valve they were intended to represent.)

Can we re-deploy our active forces from other places (variation on bringing an engine from the town behind)? Certainly, if you are willing to leave the places they now guard unguarded, give us few Reserves to respond to any other contingencies and put all our combat capability in a single place where a couple of nuclear strikes could render us militarily impotent and long-time vulnerable. What if we commit these additional forces and the Chinese decide that the time is right to move on Taiwan? Or what if the North Koreans decide that now is the time to attack South Korea? What if there is a coup in Pakistan and the Pakistanis decide to drive us out of Afghanistan?

Also consider this. Be prepared for the members of our Army to vote with their feet and leave the military in droves as soon as possible because you are granting them absolutely no personal time for normalcy with their families. Our military has risked their lives every day on multiple tours for the last three years while the rest of the country frets about who will win *Dancing with the Stars* or *American Idol.*

Can we expand our current forces so we have the necessary forces in Iraq and still guard the other places we need to guard? Certainly, but that has two drawbacks. First, getting the new soldiers up to speed will take at least as long as getting the Iraqis ready. Second, getting the number of soldiers needed probably will require an activation of the selective service system, better known as the dreaded "D" word – yes, the Draft.*

Now you know the probable reason Congressman John Murtha has gone directly to the proposal to withdraw and didn't discuss the Gorilla option. The Gorilla option means bringing up the Draft, and bringing up the Draft is the political kiss of death for the party that does so. My opinion is

---

* Another way of understanding where we are right now is to recall a scene from the movie *Top Gun*. During the final dogfight, the commander on the ship orders a back-up fighter to be launched. The commander is told the catapult is broken and will be back up in 10 minutes. "Bulls**t," the commander says. "This thing will be over in 10 minutes. Get on it." Similarly, the probability is that by the time we could draft, train and deploy more forces, the die will be cast in Iraq.

Murtha knew that the Bush Administration would not choose to go to the Draft by choice. What Murtha is saying to the Bush Administration (and to the rest of the nation) is this. Knowing that you won't do what's necessary to win, you should cut our losses. Just as in business, don't throw good money after bad. Except in war, it's not just money you lose, it's good people, as well.

By the way, I think it is amusing how Republicans and Conservatives criticize the Democrats for having "no ideas" about how to extricate ourselves honorably from Iraq. As I think I have ably demonstrated, there are no ideas worth spit. That's because the current Administration has so badly mismanaged this war. What ideas would you have if you were asked to take over a chess game that was already in checkmate? What ideas would you have if you were appointed coach for a basketball team in the fourth quarter with three minutes left to play and your team down 20 points? This is the gauntlet that the current Republican Administration, as well as the Republican-controlled Congress, is throwing down – not just to the Democrats, but to the American people. I say throw it back at them.

Why is bringing up the Draft the political kiss of death? Simply, the rules have changed from the 1960s. If the Draft comes back, there will be no exempting your children based on how much money you have. If the child's birthday is combined with a low Draft number, then the child will have the opportunity to go to Iraq and dodge the IEDs. There would be no college deferments. Personally, I would be most interested in seeing whether this nation truly has the will to fight, much less win, with a draft in place. (By the way, activating the Draft might be an interesting way to generate the manpower needed to secure our borders. The issue of a draft is worthy of discussion by itself.) But beware. A recent *Rolling Stone* magazine article reported attempts to craft a draft reinstituting exemptions for the privileged.

Why haven't you seen this kind of analysis before? I'm sure it's because those in power know to do so is to be criticized (as I'm sure I will be as an independent citizen) as soft on terror and providing aid and comfort to the enemy in time of war.

On the contrary, it is the Republicans with their bumbling and ineptitude who are providing aid and comfort to the enemy. They have fallen for the plans of Osama Bin Laden and are performing exactly to his expectations in a way that perfectly exploits our weaknesses that Bin Laden knew so well.

You're going to be told this analysis is wrong, that the Administration has things well in hand, "if we only stay the course." Use your own brain. Go back to those questions about insurgent activity and so forth. Ask yourself what makes sense to you. Ask yourself if you trust the people who said we would be greeted as liberators, the ones who said the insurgency was in its "last throes" and who blew the response to Katrina. Remember the counsel of Ralph Waldo Emerson: "What you do speaks so loud I cannot hear what you say."

So now I repeat the third question. What do we need to turn things around? Which one of these flawed options will give us the best chance to achieve our seemingly noble objectives? Who knows? I think if we can get candid answers to the following questions for **all** the options, then we will have a much clearer idea.

First, accept that what we are doing is inadequate. If you voted for Bush because you thought he and his Administration would fight for you, recognize that they are fighting poorly. Fighting poorly is probably as bad as not fighting at all.

Based on that premise, we must ask ourselves these questions:

- What do we want Iraq to look like in 10 years? What will it take for Iraq to look like that?

- If we withdraw over the horizon, will the Iraqis take care of business without involvement by our forces? (That's the tough love approach. Tough love works sometimes.)

- Do we stay and keep the engine running until some deadline date and hope the Iraqis will get out of the freight cars, attach ropes and help pull the train over the hill? Or do we take the "whatever it takes" approach and bring on the additional troops? When the insurgents add another 1,000 to their numbers, are we willing add another 10,000 to ours with all the attendant risk?

As I said, there are no good options. Answer those questions and we will know better what we as a country are willing and able to do.

Oh, and by the way – if we are short 70,000 troops to do the job in Iraq, then even if we get those troops for that job, where will we get troops (should we need them) for Iran or North Korea? For those who clamor for action on those two countries, will you clamor as loudly once the Draft is activated to get the needed troops and the young members of your family are called to fight?

One thing I do know is that I will not vote to retain in office any of those in power who have created this mess and give them additional opportunities to make things worse. I urge you to join me.

EIGHT
ABORTION

No one I know wishes there were more abortions. The common goal is fewer abortions. Unfortunately, those who would seek a complete ban on abortions are proposing something that is based on unproven religious theory rather than on proven scientific fact, fails to take into account the essentials of human nature, and, further, ignores the likely unhappy consequences of their proposal. In fact, those consequences may be expected to be even more undesirable than the current ones.

The abortion debate seems interminable. Heard the most are two arguments: Freedom of Choice advocates champion the right of a living human female to decide what happens with her own body and her own future. Pro-Life advocates believe life begins at conception; thus the destruction of the fetus is murder. These two forces will never be still, but I believe I can demonstrate a majority argument that will, like prohibition, finally set this aside as a monkey-head issue.

First of all, we need to be asking ourselves a different question about abortion:

If you, or a woman you loved, were experiencing an unwanted pregnancy that threatened her health or plans for her own life, wouldn't you want every possible option available to her to alleviate that situation (including abortion)?

You can't dismiss this question by saying an unwanted pregnancy couldn't happen to you or a woman you love. The fact is an unwanted pregnancy can happen all too easily. A pill is forgotten someday, a condom breaks or leaks or a rape occurs. When unwanted things happen in life, we must be able to deal with them.

If you're a male, I challenge you to answer that question not only for the women you love in your life, but also as if you were a woman and capable of becoming pregnant.

Let's be candid here. The only reasonable answer to my question from an intelligent, rational human being who is open to all points of view and the capabilities of medical science is yes. You might reject abortion as an option that you would personally select as a solution, but it should still be an option.

Why do I say the answer is yes? There are several reasons.

First, while I consider myself to be a spiritual person with an affiliation to a mainstream religion, I reject the theory that life begins at conception. There is no scientific proof that such is the case. The Bible itself gives service to the argument that life begins when the baby draws its first breath on its own.

Think about this comparison.

Let me place before you an egg broken in a mixing bowl, a measuring cup full of 2 cups of pancake mix and another with 1 1/3 cup of milk and say, "Eat your pancakes"? You would say I have only provided you the ingredients for pancakes, not the pancakes themselves.

So, what if I then place the batter and the milk in the bowl with the egg and mix them together and say to you again, "Eat your pancakes"? You would tell me that I have now created a pancake batter, but not actual pancakes.

So I ask you then, what does it take for you to eat your pancakes? You tell me that I have to cook the batter on a hot griddle. Only then will you consider the product to be edible.

I hope the comparison is clear to you. Just as pancakes go through a process to become pancakes (and are not pancakes until they go through that process), so must human beings go through a process to be born and actually become a human being.

Beliefs – a new view

The belief that life begins at conception is a religious belief, not a scientific fact. The attempt by religious groups to abolish abortion is an attempt to impose their religious beliefs on the entire population. The attempt to impose that religious belief by law is a violation of the American Constitution.

Let me re-state an argument I made in the introduction. In our free market system, we have any number of retailers. Let's think particularly of the so-called "big box retailers" of our time: Wal-Mart, K-Mart, JC Penney, Target, Sears, and others. Each retailer has the right to **persuade** you to shop at its store to the exclusion of the other stores. Were one of those retailers able to manipulate the political process and get laws passed so that you were **required** to shop at its store and its store only, I believe American consumers would be outraged. They would understand immediately that they were being denied the freedom of personal choice, and they were now subject to the whims of an economic monopoly. Further, they would know that monopolies are known for price fixing and price gouging – neither of which is good for them.

Our Constitution clearly allows our individual citizens to **persuade** other citizens to follow their religion over someone else's. Our Constitution just as clearly forbids the passage of laws that **require** the imposition of one group's religion onto another group. Therefore, using a religious basis to impose a ban on abortion is clearly unconstitutional.

Speaking plainly, Radical Religious Right advocates are tired of trying to convince you to adopt their philosophy. They are tired of knocking on your door and having you slam it in their face because you refuse to accept their beliefs. They hope by taking control of the political process to legislate (and therefore impose/mandate) their philosophy on you. Instead of the Radical Religious Right having to spend their personal time and funds to sell Americans on adopting their religious philosophy, they want to use taxpayer money and institutions to shove that philosophy down Americans' throats.

Going back to our criteria for monkey-head issues, we phrase our conclusion this way:

> If you or someone you love is suffering an unwanted pregnancy, then the current *Roe v. Wade* standard enables you as an abortion opponent the absolute personal freedom to reject abortion, have the child and persuade others to do likewise. This is acceptable. Enacting more restrictive laws, however, does not meet our monkey-head test.

Let me state this in a different way for those who are members of religious sects who oppose abortion. I respect your religion and its beliefs. You have a right to believe what you want to believe and to try to spread that belief through persuasion. You do not have a right to legislate that belief on non-believers. Further, I very respectfully want to suggest the following to you.

You may be rooted in a religion, but those roots do not tie you down like a tree. If a woman you loved were pregnant by virtue of a rape, would you abide by your religion's insistence that the pregnancy be carried to term? Or would you leave that religion for one with a kinder solution? I wonder what would happen if the collective membership of a religion let a demand be known to the religion's leadership. That demand would be for the religion to reconsider its position on certain sexual topics. As part of that demand, what if the membership made it known that unless changes were made the membership would take its good works elsewhere? Do you suppose a new vision might come upon the leadership, given that, without membership, there is no church?

The second reason for opposing a ban on abortion goes more directly to the criterion as to whether a monkey-head issue is acceptable or unacceptable. **Will there be any negative ripple effects from allowing this policy?** If you are able to dictate religious control over my life and the lives of the people I love on this issue, with what other aspects of life will you now meddle because you have the legal loophole to do so? Realize that the people who want to be able to meddle with your life are vocal and involved. If you want to take away the threat of their meddling, then you must make clear to the politicians who represent you that you resent this meddling and will not support politicians who support such meddling. After all, you don't want prohibition back, do you?

Some religious groups claim that because they represent the majority religion in the country, their religion should prevail. But, once again, the American Constitution clearly states that no laws shall be passed establishing a religion in this country.

Consider our other criteria questions too.

Are you (or a specific group of people already in existence who are unable to defend themselves) severely harmed by this policy in one of the following ways?

- Physically?
- Mentally/emotionally?
- Monetarily?

If you or a woman you love is suffering from an unwanted pregnancy, then an abortion ban that keeps you from having a wanted abortion will clearly harm you physically, mentally, emotionally and monetarily. You are harmed physically, because you must endure the pain of childbirth (which is adding insult to injury if your pregnancy is the result of a rape). You are harmed mentally and emotionally, because you must rearrange the plans for your life to accommodate this unwanted child (and especially if the reason for the pregnancy is rape or incest). You are harmed financially, because someone else has mandated that you bear the expense of birthing the child and (if you raise the child yourself instead of seeking adoption) raising the child to adulthood.

Let's review that same criterion if you yourself are not involved in the pregnancy or the abortion. You are not harmed physically by what takes place with another person. You may suffer some emotional and mental stress that such is occurring and you may wish it were not. So do many of us. But your own emotional and mental stress is not equal to that of the woman actually experiencing the pregnancy, so her stress must take precedence over yours. Financially, you are unlikely to be harmed if the abortion takes place, but you may be harmed if the abortion does not take place. We'll talk to that point in a moment.

An ounce of prevention

Let's talk about some of the other negative ripple effects from a ban on abortion and some of the related aspects to this issue. For example, what about efforts to reduce funding for family planning services and supplies in this country and abroad? Do we truly think that enabling the continuance of ignorance is a way to reduce unwanted pregnancies? Is this in keeping with Benjamin Franklin's saying, "An ounce of prevention is worth a pound of cure"? Does it serve us to continue with ignorance of AIDS (Acquired Immunodeficiency Syndrome) in Africa? Does it serve us to have a nation of poverty-stricken orphans because we are unwilling to provide contraceptives to those who need and can't afford them?

An effort to restrict abortion through denial of contraceptives reveals a repressive attitude toward sex itself. Do advocates of this approach seriously think they can lessen the desire for sex by these means? I'm reminded of a conversation with an Army commander. His organization had both male and female soldiers living in a barracks with a co-ed dormitory-like environment. Because my own experience was with male-only organizations, I asked the commander how he was handling the potential of sexual activity among the soldiers in his barracks. He shook his head and gave me a reply that the present day Puritans in our society should take to heart. The commander said, "You ain't (sic) never gonna stop he-in' and she-in', and I'm not going to waste my time trying." In other words, as long as what went on was done between consenting adults and was not done among people who worked for (as opposed to with) one another, what did he care? He had more important issues that took priority.

Ask yourself: Do you prefer hot cooked food to cold, raw uncooked food? Chances are you do. You realize, of course, cooking carries with it exposure to heated stoves, ovens and cooking implements. Does the possibility of getting burned keep you from cooking? No, you simply take precautions. You grab pans by their handles. You use oven mitts and pot holders. I'm sure occasionally you have made a mistake and burned yourself. Did that stop you from cooking? No, you just reinforced the safety rules for yourself and went on.

Aren't the same things true about sex? As a consenting adult, don't you like sex? I believe the following quote is from Helen Gurley Brown. "Sex is one of the three great adult pleasures . . . and I can't remember what the other two are." If you make a mistake and burn yourself, should you be forced to let the wound fester or should you be allowed to get the medical treatment you need? (Please don't tell me abortions are the result of promiscuous lifestyles. Studies show that three of 10 unwanted pregnancies come in wedlock. Avoiding pregnancy over a 20- to 30-year time period while the female partner is fertile and still maintaining sexual vitality in the relationship is no easy task.)

One other ripple effect, however, needs to be explored. Quite often, those who seek to ban abortions are also highly motivated by another topic. That topic is the prospect of reducing the size of government, which, therefore, reduces taxes. Let's look at what might happen if a ban were in effect.

Recognize first if a ban were in effect many unwanted children would be born. Now recognize that the reasons for abortions being done are several. One, the potential child was unwanted due to the personal plans of the couple involved. Second, the potential child was wanted, but unaffordable because of the cost of the medical procedure or the costs of raising the child (which speaks to health care costs and the number of medically uninsured in this country, but that's another topic.) A variation of the second reason would be that a medical condition of the mother or the fetus was such that continuing the pregnancy was too risky. Currently, the number of abortions in the U.S. per year has been averaging about 1.3 million.

Abortion as a cost savings

What this means, then, is if abortion were banned, every year about 1.3 million children could be coming unwanted into this society. Some would be absorbed by adoption, but a significant portion of those would likely end up in our foster care system. What percentage? Who knows, but remember these are unwanted children. Why don't we use 20 percent to calculate an example? So 20 percent of 1.3 million is 260,000. The estimated annual cost of a child in foster care is $30,000, so I've been told. Multiplying 260,000 (the number of children) by $30,000 (the annual cost of their care) is $7.80 billion. If every year another 260,000 unwanted children are added to the system, then in 10 years the total cost would become $78 billion per year and growing. At age 18 those in foster care would leave the program, so this would be the peak of the program at over $140 billion per year. That's $140 billion in additional taxes for all of us to share because certain religious groups want to impose their religious beliefs on the rest of us.

The cost to society may well continue after the child turns 18. That's because, regardless of whether a child is adopted, sent to foster care, or remains with their birth parents, children born in these circumstances may be more likely to be a burden to society with regard to welfare or crime or both. Estimates are that an individual in prison costs society $61 a day in direct costs. In the $61 we are not counting the wages this person might have earned and the taxes they would have paid as a contributing member of society. That's $61 multiplied by 365 days equals an annual cost of $22,265. If 5 percent of this additional population ends up in jail, we will have an additional 65,000 people in jail every year after the 18th year. In 10 years, that's 650,000 people in prison at a cost of $22,265 each (not allowing for inflation, assuming they all served 10-year sentences or more). That's an additional cost of over $4.8 billion a year in taxes.

Now, of course, someone might argue back that my predicted negative percentages are too high and that there are additional people born to help defray those costs. That might be true, but what if my assumptions are wrong by being too conservative? What if twice as many unwanted children require foster care? Three times as many? Double or triple the estimated number of those requiring imprisonment and tell me if you like what those numbers tell you about tax costs. Especially when those costs are avoidable.

There is historical precedent validating what I'm saying about abortion as a cost savings. In the book *Freakonomics*, the authors demonstrate the statistical validity of the fact that the existence of *Roe v. Wade* helped avert a crime wave in the 1990s with its increased losses to society and increased prison costs before it happened. Why? Because the angry young men who would have made that crime wave happen were not born into the circumstances that would have produced them.

I have had the thought that one way to settle once and for all the question of legalized abortion might be to have a national referendum. Since there is no other mechanism for doing this (even the election of the President is not decided by the popular vote), I think it might be interesting to do this. Let's have check-off boxes on our federal income tax returns to vote for or against legalized abortion, but with one minor point attached. If you check the box that you want to ban legalized abortion, then you also agree to pay an additional 5 percent of your adjusted gross income into a fund to defray the costs unwanted births will bring to our society. Further you agree that your spouse, your children (remember their social security numbers are on the tax return), your children's children and their children's children will be subject to this surtax for the next 100 years or until such time as abortion is legalized again. If you vote no, then even if a ban is voted in, you don't have to pay the additional 5 percent.

What a great way to get those who oppose abortion to literally "put their money where their mouth is." If those who oppose abortion win, then they get what they want socially, but it does not affect those who want abortion to be legal as strongly financially.

One more comment for the benefit of you who think you are doing God's will by opposing abortion. The syndicated columnist, author and humorist Lewis Grizzard used to tell this story about the preacher whose house is flooding:

> The preacher's house was down by the river and the river is beginning to flood its banks. Some men drive by in a pickup truck and call to the preacher sitting on his front porch.
>
> "Preacher," they say. "That water is rising fast. You better come with us." The preacher replies, "No, boys, I'll be fine. The Lord will take care of me."
>
> Some hours later, the men come back in a rowboat. By this time the preacher is sitting on the roof of his front porch to avoid the rising water. "Preacher," they say again. "That water is rising fast. You better come with us." The preacher replies, "No, boys, I'll be fine. The Lord will take care of me."
>
> Still later, the men come back again in a helicopter to find the preacher clinging to the chimney of his house to keep from being swept away into the raging water. "Preacher," they say yet again. "That water is rising fast. You better come with us." The preacher replies, "No, boys, I'll be fine. The Lord will take care of me."
>
> Suddenly, the preacher found himself at the Pearly Gates. Saint Peter, seeing the preacher, says to him, "What are you doing here? It ain't your time." The preacher replies, "I don't know. I thought you would take care of me."
>
> Saint Peter says, "Shoot, I sent a pickup truck, a rowboat and a helicopter. What do you want?"

Funny story, you might say. But what does that have to do with abortion? Simply this. What if one of the ministers who has advocated a ban on abortion and contraceptives appears at the Pearly Gates? Expecting a reward for his advocacy, he or she says to Saint Peter, "I did my best to stop abortion like you wanted."

Saint Peter replies, "How did you know what God wanted? God was trying to create less pain for those on earth and to get the right mix of people on the planet so she could take the next steps in her plan. So she sent legalized abortion, contraception and the morning-after pill. But certain people kept interfering with her plan by opposing access to those things. What kind of reward do you think God ought to provide to someone who actively opposed her plan?"

Different perspective, isn't it?

Overall, I think I have demonstrated to you that the continued legalization of abortion is the course of action that does the most good for the greatest amount of people and the least damage to the fewest number of people. It is the best we can do with the funds available given competing priorities and it does the best job of avoiding unintended ripple effects. Further, legalized abortion is in keeping with our goals of limited government, social tolerance and fiscal responsibility.

How to take action

If you agree with my analysis of this issue, then this is what I recommend you do when you write your letter to the political powers that be. Let them know that:

- You recommend that abortion remain a legal choice in this country.

- You think the argument used by the Radical Religious Right to justify the outlawing of abortion is a religious one and that using that argument to amend the law is, in your opinion, unconstitutional.

- You think there is more support for this book's position than for that of the Radical Religious Right. Elected officials should not be intimidated by the outspoken opposition of the Radical Religious Right.

The other reason you support continued legalization of abortion is the potential for increased taxation burdens on society if abortion were no longer legal. You encourage your representative to use that projection with Pro-Life constituents.

You recommend that officials confirm that pro-abortion support is the majority position by polling with questions like the following: If you, or a woman you loved, were experiencing an unwanted pregnancy, which threatened her health and/or plans for her own life, would you want every possible option available to alleviate that situation (including abortion)? (If you're a man being asked this question, please answer that question for yourself as though you were capable of becoming pregnant.)

Would you be in favor of paying increased taxes to defray the additional costs to society from imposing a ban on abortion?

✓

NINE
GAY MARRIAGE

Why do some heterosexuals feel their marriage will be threatened or cheapened if two people of the same sex are married? I really am perplexed by this. I have lived long enough and visited enough places both in the U.S. and Europe to know what I prefer isn't always for everyone else. I don't care as long as the two (or more) of the parties who are being married are capable of having assigned social security numbers.

Here is what I have discovered for myself. Many reasons are given, spoken or unspoken, that people offer for opposing gay marriage. One of the best summaries of those reasons I found was a Web site by Scott Bidstrup at **www.bidstrup.com/marriage.htm**. I will comment on only one of those reasons. And that's the one in which some people feel exposing children to a homosexual household is wrong. Well, was it wrong for a homosexual child to be raised in the heterosexual household that produced the child? There seems to be some expectation that homosexual parents will teach a child to be a homosexual and how to have homosexual sex.

If that's what you think, then I want all you heterosexuals to imagine the same concept for your own household. Imagine Dad standing outside the bedroom with an erection and Mom inside the bedroom "nekkid" (as Lewis Grizzard used to say – his devoted fans will know what I mean). Dad calls out, "You kids get in here. Your Ma and I got something to show you."

Never would happen, right? Well, never say never; there is always the 1 percent somewhere who will do the unexpected. Still, in general, for sex to occur for most people it must be done in private with a setting and a mood established. The interruption by additional people can be really deflating (pardon the pun). In fact, I remember reading a story about a divorced man who spoke of his previous married life and how remarkable it was that married couples had more children after the first one because of the interruptions the first child caused at critical moments.

All this aside, let's analyze gay marriage using our methodology. **Will there be any negative ripple effects from allowing gay marriage?** Opponents to gay marriage might say there are several. Those include the potential for bestiality or for children to be subject to child abuse. To the former I say write the statute so that marriage is between human beings. That way we can avoid someone claiming their pet dog as a deduction on their income tax. As to child abuse, I think some people confuse homosexuality with pedophilia. I simply see no rational connection between homosexuality and a propensity for child abuse. Do some homosexuals abuse children? Yes, but so do some heterosexuals. If we are truly concerned about children, then perhaps we need to do a better job of educating people to be parents and somehow screening those who wish to have children for indications of potential abusive behavior.

Are you (or a specific group of people already in existence who are unable to defend themselves) severely harmed by this policy in one of the following ways?

- Physically?
- Mentally/ emotionally?
- Monetarily?

You are not personally harmed physically in your person or in your property by a gay marriage any more than you are by a new heterosexual marriage.

You may claim to be mentally/emotionally harmed by your distaste for the existence of the marriage. But the fact is that you are not being directly insulted as if someone were yelling profanities in your face. Let me use a food example. Maybe you can't stand the taste of liver, but are you mentally/emotionally harmed if you observe someone else eating liver? No, you are not. So, in the same way, your revulsion toward the acts of two consenting adults does not affect you.

In fact, isn't it time you admitted to yourself that the real reason for your opposition to gay marriage is based on your physical revulsion? Someone out there is going to claim a moral argument that the Bible condemns homosexuality.

Clearly, I've used a couple of Biblical passages here myself I thought appropriate to my argument. That doesn't mean that literal interpretations of the Bible are always applicable. Doesn't the Bible say having slaves is okay as long as those slaves are from another country? So, I'm sorry, but I can't accept your Biblical argument.

What effect does gay marriage have on you monetarily? Can your bank accounts be raided? Is your house somehow devalued because two gay people chose to get married? Does the stock you own go down in value because two gay people choose to publicly declare their lasting affection for one another? The answers are no, aren't they?

Moreover, which issue is truly more likely to affect your well being?

- Gay marriage or terrorism?
- Gay marriage or the state of the economy?
- Gay marriage or the cost of health care?
- Gay marriage or illegal immigration?

Gay marriage didn't win a single time, did it? So which issues do you want to take the time of your elected representatives? My answer is that we should let gay people have what they want (and deserve, in my opinion) and move on to the issues that truly threaten our well being. This solution does the most good for the greatest amount of people, with the least damage to the fewest number of people, and is financially sound with no discernible ripple effects. Further, this solution is in keeping with our goals of limited government, social tolerance and fiscal prudence.

PART III
TAKE ACTION: A PROPOSED LETTER FOR YOU TO WRITE

If you'll recall, at the beginning of this book, I stated:

"If enough people like you read this book, agree with the principles proposed by the book and tell the political parties that the one of them that offers policies and candidates in agreement with those principles will be the one you vote for, then the political parties must either act to become dominant or be dominated."

Part Three of this book gives you a way to tell the political parties what you think. I offer a suggested format for the letters I recommend you write.

Earlier I also pointed out:

"I do not expect that you will agree with me 100 percent on all those positions."

The format of the letter allows for your disagreement with or modification of what I have written. The key is this. If you want to see a change in how politics is done in this country, then you must write. The zealots in this country want to see the prohibition type issues stay on the table. You can be sure they will write and oppose the proposals I have in this book. If the only people the political parties hear from are the zealots, then business as usual will continue. If you agree with the philosophy and concepts I have shown you, if you want a change in how this country does its political business, then write the letters I recommend. Let the political powers know what you want and that you will support change in concert with the philosophy and concepts of this book.

Show other people you know this book. Request they read it and write their own letters. Don't continue to sit silently at home unless you are satisfied with how things are politically and want them to continue.

That said, let's talk about who to contact and how to contact them.

There are two ways for you to communicate with the people I will recommend you contact. One is regular U.S. mail. The other is email. Regardless of which you choose, I would like to know what you had to say. If you would then, please, send me a copy of what you write.

The address to use with U.S. mail is as follows:
Kindred Minds Enterprises
663 N. 132nd Street Ste 125
Omaha, NE 68154

Copy your email to me at **Author@kindredmindsent.com**.

Here are the people and offices I suggest you write to:

- The leaders of both the Republican and Democratic parties (both the National and your State leaders)

- The heads of other political parties, such as the Libertarian and Green parties

- The Governor of your state

- Your State Senator

- Your State Legislative Representative

- Your Representative in the U.S. House of Representatives

- Both your State's Senators in the U.S. Senate

There are several ways to find the physical or email addresses you need. One is to look at **www.firstgov.org**.

The government pages of your local phone directory will offer addresses and phone numbers. You can then call to get email addresses.

Here is the data for the Republicans. From there you can drill down to your state party representatives.

> Republican National Committee
> 310 First Street, SE
> Washington, DC 20003
> 202.863.8500
> Email: **info@gop.com**

And here is the data for the Democrats. Again, their site will enable you to drill down to the data for the state party representatives.

> Democratic National Committee
> 430 S. Capitol St. SE
> Washington, DC 20003
> Email: See this link:
> **www.democrats.org/page/s/contact**

You can find the other political parties using Internet search engines.

And, of course, if all else fails your trusty local reference librarian can help you.

A copy of the suggested letter is available on my Web site in a format for you to copy and paste.

Thank you for reading my book. I hope you found its contents clarifying and enlightening.

Please share the book with others so that good efficient limited government based on fiscal responsibility and social tolerance can be a reality in this country as rapidly as possible.

Suggested Letter Format

Your Name
Your Street Address
Your City, State and Zip

Date

Name of the Organization
Street Address
City, State, Zip

Good Afternoon:

I recently read the book *Neither Liberal Nor Conservative Be*. I respectfully request you and the members of your party strongly consider adopting its philosophy.

The author wrote this book because he was disgusted by the unending confrontational nature of polarized American politics. He was furious with the approaches taken to solve our national issues. So am I.

He asks in the book if, at election time, I feel forced to choose between the lesser of two evils. He asks if I find myself asking, "Is **this** the best we can do?" I have to say what he wrote is how I feel and what I ask myself.

This book is an open letter to the political parties in the United States of America. The book is written in much the same way that you might write a letter to car makers who are not producing a car you are willing to buy. While you might not expect that one of them will give you 100 percent of what you want, you would hope that one of them could give you 85 to 90 percent of your needs. In the same way, neither of the major political parties is promoting the policies and candidates or taking the actions I agree with 85 to 90 percent. This book offers your party an opinion of what you must offer me in order to consistently receive my vote. I agreed with enough of what this book has to say to write you and tell you this is what I'm looking for. I didn't agree with everything and I'll tell you more about that in a moment.

Here's what the book teaches that I agree with.

- Too much of politics is made up of manipulative language and issues. I will not vote for someone who tries to manipulate me. For my part, I pledge to be more informed so that I am not easily influenced by 30-second commercials.

- I expect you to earn my vote by explaining how issues affect this nation and its citizens both individually and collectively. Analyze the issues by explaining their impact on me physically, mentally/emotionally and financially. Before you make proposals make sure that you have completely analyzed those proposals and can assure me the ripple effects of implementing those proposals will not leave me worse off than the problem the proposal was intended to solve.

- Govern with the goal of making policy to simultaneously achieve three things: limited government, fiscal responsibility and social tolerance.

- Analyze issues and create solutions that keep the following in mind: **Does this solution serve the largest number of people for the longest period of time as balanced against doing the least harm or disruption to the fewest number of people and is it the best solution monetarily we can get for the funds available among competing priorities?**

- Among the things keeping us from solving our problems are some societal issues that are the equivalent of slavery and prohibition. We have reached the point where we need to

establish an acceptable solution that will take
these issues off the table and move forward.

- Finally, I want you to get away from the issue
  orientation we have today. I want you to
  re-orient toward goals and a vision for where
  this country needs to be 5, 10, 20 years from.

I want to mention the following points that also
made an impact on me (insert your thoughts here):

I told you I did not agree with everything. Here is
how I would modify some of the author's
proposals (insert your thoughts here):

I appreciate your attention to my letter and the
service you provide through your office. I hope
that you and the other members of your party will
be persuaded, as I am, that the approach provided
in *Neither Liberal Nor Conservative Be* offers a way
for us to resolve many of our long-standing issues
in this country and truly begin to make progress
for ourselves and our children.

You can contact me through the data I've provided
in this letter. The book can be obtained through
the my Web site, **www.KindredMindsEnt.com**.

Very Respectfully,
Your Name
Your Phone Number

Resources

How to Have a Discussion Instead of an Argument

In this section will give you some ideas and suggestions about how to have a civil discussion with someone. These ideas and suggestions particularly apply when the person you are trying to have a reasoned discussion with is a zealot with radical views.

You may have seen this saying with another word substituted for the word *zealot*, but the saying certainly applies. Arguing with a zealot is like wrestling with a pig. You both get dirty, but the pig loves it.

I offer you here some specific techniques and approaches you can use. Just as I suggested you might want to partner up with someone who shares your views to see what both sides are saying, you may also want to practice some of this dialogue at home in a safe environment before attempting it in a live situation.

The key to avoiding arguments is to use a third-party approach. That means that instead of you making an argument as if it were your own, you make it on behalf of someone else. You act as though you are simply curious to see what the person who was holding forth so passionately would have to say to this third party. This approach requires you to develop a new way of speaking similar to what you would have to do if you were playing a home version of the popular television game show, *Jeopardy*.

As you probably know, *Jeopardy* requires you to provide information by asking a question. For example, the clue might be, "The 40th President of the United States." Your "answer" would be, "Who is Ronald Reagan?"

Similarly, let's imagine you at a party standing with a group of people and someone decides to go off on a rant about some particular topic. Your opinion about that topic disagrees with the one being voiced. You could start off with something like, "You are so full of it." And then you are off to the races with a full-blown argument.

Try this instead. What if you said to the person voicing strong opinions, "That's very interesting. Tell me what you would say to someone who said, "[state your Jeopardy question]" and then state the case as you know it. Now when the first person replies to you, they are not replying to you directly. The person, therefore, is not arguing with you directly. They are debating this mythical third person and their ideas.

Without a third party being physically present, the speaker is unable to personalize the debate by attacking the person instead of their ideas. If the speaker does try the distraction of personalizing the debate, then that says that the speaker has not thought through both sides of the issue and is trying to avoid revealing that fact by avoiding the question.

If the speaker does try to personalize the debate, then you can respond to the speaker by saying something to this effect, "I really have no idea about what kind of person might have the idea I just shared with you, but I was hoping you would give me your thoughts on the ideas themselves." The individual who is unable to respond will realize the fact that they probably don't have the complete insight they need on the matter in question.

Another way to begin a third-party presentation is to use the content of this book. If the speaker is talking about something you disagree with because of reading this book, then you can do the following. Ask the speaker if they have read *Neither Liberal Nor Conservative Be*. If the person says yes, then you can ask them what they think of the reasoning described in the book. If they have read the book, then you should be able to have a reasoned discussion.

If the person says they haven't read the book, then you can recommend that they read it and then come back to you for discussion. If the person presses you to describe the reasoning in the book, then you have the option to describe the reasoning yourself or to say that you don't think you can do the ideas justice and suggest again the other person read the book. That way you avoid confrontation and you contribute to reasoned dialogue and education leading to consensus rather than conflict. (You may find this technique particularly useful in dealing with people whose means of discussing political issues is repeating the confrontational language they've heard on radio and television.)

Yet another way to use the philosophy of the book might be as follows. This may be useful if the speaker is talking about a topic you haven't fully developed a position for. In this case, you might want to ask the speaker a series of questions.

- "You seem very strong about what you're talking about here. May I ask you a couple of questions about this topic?"

- "Are you so passionate about this because it affects you personally in some physical way?" (If yes, ask "how so"? and keep probing and asking them to talk.)

- "Are you so passionate about this because it affects you personally in some mental or emotional way?" (If yes, ask "how so"? and keep probing, asking them to talk.)

- "Are you so passionate about this because it affects you personally in some financial way?" (If yes, ask "how so"? and keep probing and asking them to talk.)

- "If we were to take your approach, can you think of any negative ripple effects of doing it that way?" (If they can't think of any and you can, bring yours up. "What would you do if this happens as a result of doing what you want to do here?")

- "If we were to take your approach, can you think of any precedents we would be setting that would allow other things to happen that we wouldn't want to happen?" (If they can't think of any and you can, bring yours up. "What would you do if this happens as a result of doing what you want to do here?")

A good summary might be, "Well, if this doesn't affect you personally, physically, mentally, emotionally or financially and the impact of doing what you want to do has other consequences you don't want, then do you still feel this strongly about this topic?"

This approach may also reveal to you that your own thoughts about a particular topic aren't thorough enough. Remember to say to yourself, "I may be wrong. I often am."

Letter from the Author to the Political VIPs

Larry R. Bradley
Kindred Minds Publishing
Omaha, Nebraska

Date
Various Political Luminaries

Good Afternoon:

I am enclosing a copy of the book *Neither Liberal Nor Conservative Be* and request that you and the members of your party strongly consider adopting its philosophy.

I wrote this book because I am disgusted by the unending confrontational nature of polarized American politics. I am furious with the approaches taken to solve our national issues.

In the voting booth, I feel forced to choose between the lesser of two evils. I find myself asking, "Is **this** the best we can do?"

This book is an open letter to the political parties in the United States of America. I am writing this letter in the same way I might write a letter to car makers who are not producing a car I am willing to buy. While I might not expect that one of them will give me 100 percent of the features I want, I would hope one of them could meet 85 to 90 percent of my needs.

In the same way, neither of the major political parties is promoting the policies and candidates I can have 85 to 90 percent agreement with. The book offers the parties my opinion of what they must offer me in order to consistently receive my vote. My goal and hope is that other Americans will join me in telling you this is the kind of politics and government they want too.

The details of my proposals are in my book. You may also contact me through my Web site, **www.KindredMindsEnt.com**.

I appreciate your attention to my letter and the service you provide through your office. I hope that you and the other members of your party will be persuaded, as I am, that the approach provided in *Neither Liberal Nor Conservative Be* offers a way for us to resolve many of our long-standing issues in this country and truly begin to make progress for ourselves and our children.

Very Respectfully,
Larry R. Bradley

Index

About the Author

Larry R. Bradley is a native of Missouri. He began his adult work life by accompanying his undergraduate degree in Political Science from Missouri State University with a commission as a Regular Army Infantry Officer. During his Army career, Larry also earned an MBA in Management from the University of Tennessee.

Larry split his military career between combat units (with a preference for Mechanized Infantry and Armor) and Research and Development (R&D) activities. His combat unit assignments include commanding a Mechanized Infantry unit in Europe.

His involvement in R&D (the business side of the Army) gave him a unique perspective into the political and economic dynamics of military procurement and national defense. Larry's assignments in this area began with the initial fielding of the Bradley Fighting Vehicle System to the Army at Fort Hood, TX. Later, while at the Headquarters of the Training and Doctrine Command at Fort Monroe, VA, he co-authored the Army's revised policy on modifications to Army equipment (a part of Army operations with a price tag at the time as high as $36 Billion).

Following his military career, Larry established a second career for himself in sales. Besides the numerous awards and esteem Larry gathered from his efforts, his influence and impact was probably best reflected by the nickname conferred upon him by his superiors, peers and subordinates at a Fortune 500 company: the "Doctor of Sales".

Widowed unexpectedly, Larry has two adult daughters by that marriage. Through the wonders of an Internet dating service, Larry made what he describes as a "10 million to one shot" when he met his current wife in late 2001. They live in Omaha, NE.

Larry's passion for the future well being of the country he served so long and his concern for the direction he saw that country taking caused him to found Kindred Minds Enterprises and write Neither Liberal Nor Conservative Be.